SANCTIFY
THEM
IN
TRUTH

SANCTIFY THEM IN TRUTH

How the Church's Social Doctrine Addresses the Issues of Our Time

Fr. Jeffrey Kirby, STD

TAN Books
Gastonia, North Carolina

Cover design by David Ferris—www.davidferrisdesign.com

Cover image:

Library of Congress Control Number: 2021951933

ISBN: 978-1-5051-2113-1
Kindle ISBN: 978-1-5051-2114-8
ePUB ISBN: 978-1-5051-2115-5

Published in the United States by
TAN Books
PO Box 269
Gastonia, NC 28053
www.TANBooks.com

To my beloved sister, Melanie Kirby-McDaniel

Contents

Introduction

"I Kept Checking . . ."

Years ago, Pope Benedict XVI welcomed former Anglican and Episcopalian clergy into the Catholic priesthood through a specially designed personal prelature. At the time, I was fortunate enough to meet and get to know several of these new Catholic priests. It was a joy and encouragement to hear the diverse stories of how God led each one of these respective men into the Catholic Church and its ordained priesthood.

One new priest recounted how his growing appreciation of the Church's social doctrine led him to ask several life-changing questions. As he described it, as an Episcopalian priest, his parishioners would often approach him about current issues and ask what the biblical or Christian response was to such contemporary challenges. In his search for guidance, he realized there was very little theological assistance in his own tradition. He wondered, "How can we not have a teaching on this question?"

His search for answers would often lead him to the teachings of the Catholic Church. He remarked, "It seemed only the Catholic Church was concerned about showing believers how to live as Christians in the twenty-first century." Many times, he would literally hide a copy of the *Catechism of the Catholic Church* under his desk. "I kept checking on what the Catholic Church was teaching."

Eventually, this unintended, but repeated, journey into the social teachings of the Church led him to ask some sincere and life-altering questions. And, of course, the rest is history, as he's now a Roman Catholic and serves as one of our priests. The experience of this one priest shows us the depth and breadth of the Church's magisterial teachings, especially in terms of social doctrine.

Do we appreciate the Church's social doctrine in our own lives? Have we explored its richness as we try to live Christian lives in our world today?

Why This Book?

This book is provided as help to Christian believers in learning and appreciating the social doctrine of the Church. Regrettably, the social doctrine—which is the application of the Church's dogmatic doctrine to society and its issues—has been called Christianity's "best kept secret." Yet the Church's teachings on social issues shouldn't be a secret to anyone, especially to believers. It is imperative that Christians today know how to answer the various social questions and concerns of our day.

And so, this book serves as a resource and outline on how to initiate conversations and answer the questions and concerns of our day, both intellectually and spiritually.

Knowing these answers are important for several reasons. In particular, three such reasons stand out:

1. The Christian answers to our social questions today are reflections of the wisdom and power of the Gospel and divine revelation. It is a source of life and a sure guide on how to live well and love honestly.

2. The Christian answers to our social concerns provide us with the best structure for a civilized society, a strong community life, and robust civic friendship.

3. Christian believers have been passive and silent for too long on societal issues. They have allowed themselves to be shamed and have accepted the lie of a privatization of religion. It is time for believers to find their voice (and their backbones).

With that said, let's look at some of the social issues that have been selected for this book.

The Issues of Our Day

In assessing the social issues that are raised in pastoral and other circumstances, the following eight have been selected for this book. While each of them relies on multiple principles and virtues, two main principles of our social doctrine and one virtue from our moral tradition have been selected for each issue. The respective principles and virtue were chosen because of the help they give in understanding the issue at hand.

These specific issues have been chosen because of how frequently they're brought up in conversations, their significance in understanding the Christian faith, and the popularity of their subject matter in the prevailing culture. These are the selected issues:

- Abortion and Preeminence
- Immigration and Prudence
- The Environment and Stewardship
- The LGBTQ+ Movement and Complementarity
- Universal Healthcare and Subsidiarity
- Artificial Nutrition/Hydration and Mercy
- Critical Race Theory and Justice
- The Male Priesthood and Gender Equality

Each of these issues will be explored in their own chapter, with a thorough answer from the perspective of the Christian faith provided and developed for each.

While the Church has many avenues for her social teachings, such as the *Compendium of the Social Doctrine of the Church*, numerous papal encyclicals and exhortations, as well as decrees and instructions from the various dicasteries of the Vatican, the answers provided in this book are based predominantly on the *Catechism of the Catholic Church* (*CCC*). Such an approach was chosen so as to help the reader understand the basics of the respective teachings as well as to highlight the invaluable resource of the *Catechism*. Such a focused approach also makes it easier for the reader to check the quoted material and pursue additional studies in the area.

In addition, spiritual resources will be given in each chapter.

Structure of the Chapters

Since each social issue has its own chapter, each chapter will follow a set guideline. This guideline is provided as help to the reader in preparing for the argument, presenting the argument, and then following up the argument with a spiritual response. Each chapter consists, therefore, of three main parts:

1. *Building a Foundation:* This part of the chapter presents both a virtue and some guiding principles from the Church's social doctrine. Without such help, we run the risk of relying on a misguided conscience or on mere sentiment. Emotion runs high when social issues are raised, so it's important that we direct both our emotions and conscience according to truth and goodness.

2. *Taking Our Stand:* This part of the chapter presents the teachings on the specific issue, along with some key takeaways on the issue in question. It is important that our arguments are reasonable, organized, and systematic. We always want a presentation of moral truth to be consistent, credible, and convincing.

3. *Going to the Mountain:* In this concluding section, we ask God's blessings upon us, and upon all those with whom we've had conversations or arguments. We offer petitions to God as we desire to share the truths of faith with all men and women of goodwill. As such, this part of the chapter presents resources for our spiritual life.

With this structure in mind, we're ready to begin.

Time to Begin!

As we conclude this introduction, we are now ready to dive into the social issues selected for this book. The reader is free to move through them in order, skip around as needed, or go directly to a selected chapter for guidance.

As we begin our exploration of the questions of our day, the exhortation of Saint Peter is given to all: "Always be prepared to make a defense to any one who calls you to account for the hope that is in you, yet do it with gentleness and reverence; and keep your conscience clear, so that, when you are abused, those who revile you for your good behavior in Christ may be put to shame" (1 Pt 3:15–16).

CHAPTER 1

Abortion and Preeminence

*"When Elizabeth heard the greeting of Mary, the babe leaped
in her womb; and Elizabeth was filled with the Holy Spirit."*
—Luke 1:41

Building a Foundation

B*efore we present the issue of abortion, it's critical that we
have a sense of virtue and some guiding principles from the
Church's social doctrine.*

VIRTUE: *FORTITUDE*
(SEE *CCC* 1808)

Fortitude is a high moral virtue. It strengthens the human
will and empowers it to face difficulties and struggles with
resolution and purpose. Fortitude gives rectitude to a person.
It resists temptations that threaten truth, beauty, or goodness. Fortitude enables a person to overcome fear, human
respect, and vainglory. It allows a person to accept trials and
persecutions, and even death, for the sake of what is right
and true.

PRINCIPLE: *PREEMINENCE*
(SEE *CCC* 90, 2270, 2273)

Preeminence is the term used to describe the highest of truths within the hierarchy of moral truths. It distinguishes an intrinsically evil act from a prudential one while also acknowledging an order among intrinsic issues. As such, the term is used exclusively for the horror of abortion, emphasizing the issue's priority over all other related life or social issues. Abortion is preeminent among all life and social issues since it directly attacks life in its initial and most vulnerable state.

A SECOND PRINCIPLE: *NATURAL RIGHTS*
(SEE *CCC* 1928–48)

Natural rights are given by God and imbedded into human nature. They precede society and government. They are not given by any human authority. A person does not even give natural rights to himself and, therefore, cannot take them from himself. Natural rights are universal and held by every human person. Such rights must be respected by society's laws, public policies, and popular customs. Laws that violate or deny natural rights are unjust laws. Governments that offend or reject natural rights undermine their own moral legitimacy to govern.

Taking Our Stand

Since we have the assistance of virtue and principles from the Church's social doctrine, we are now ready to dive into the question of abortion and preeminence.

"I Thought I Understood . . ."

Some time ago, a young couple reached out to me about baptizing their child. We set up the appointment, and things seemed to be in place. When they arrived, there was no baby. I was a little surprised, but sometimes parents keep the little one with loved ones when they come to such appointments.

When I inquired about it, they said, "Oh, the baby hasn't been born yet." Of course, you would have thought I had noticed that fact, but I have learned not to notice or comment on the physique of women. And so, I gently asked them, "Are you expecting a difficult pregnancy?" They were shocked: "Father, no, everything is going very smoothly." I was more than confused at this point and asked, "Okay, then help me understand: why are we scheduling the baby's baptism before the child is born?"

From the pocket of his slacks, the father took out an ultrasound picture of the preborn child. It was then clear to me that this was their first child, since things like this happen with the first one. He was very excited about the future birth of his child. He wanted to schedule everything as if this was the first baby in human history. And for him, it was. This was his child. Their child.

As he showed me the ultrasound picture, he was moved by the image. "I thought I understood that life was precious and that it started in the womb, but now I truly realize what that all means. Look at this picture! This is my son!" The conversation continued with the usual jubilation over the anticipation of a child.

This account can help us all to truly realize—and not simply "know"—the innocence and dignity, the beauty and the invaluable nature of life, particularly life in the womb, at its genesis. This sensitivity and awareness is essential as we move forward and discuss abortion and the principle of preeminence.

> "If you want equal justice for all, and true freedom and lasting peace, then, America, defend life! All the great causes that are yours today will have meaning only to the extent that you guarantee the right to life and protest the human person."
>
> —Pope Saint John Paul II, Airport Address,
> Denver, CO, World Youth Day 1993

The Evil of Abortion

Embryology is clear, as is all of its related medical sciences, that life begins at conception. There is no question about this statement when it comes to the empirical sciences. This is a fact. Since life begins at conception, the smallest of human beings share in the rights and privileges of every other human person. This is good logic, sound legal theory, and an affirmation of universal human rights.

As such, abortion is a direct attack on life, its dignity, and on the normative standards of what it means to be a part of a civilized society. Abortion is an assault on life in its earliest, most vulnerable, and defenseless state. It is a barbaric act devoid of any moral or human sense. Abortion, therefore, is intrinsically evil, which means it is absolutely evil. It is never permitted or justified under any situation. No intention or circumstance, no prudential judgment, can ever make it morally acceptable.

Abortion is particularly egregious since the accomplice who is empowering the aggressor is the mother (and in many cases also the father) of the child. Still more, you have a medical doctor under an oath to "do no harm." These two positions—the parents and the doctor—are some of the most sacrosanct vocations in human society, and yet—in the horrendous act of abortion—they conspire to destroy an innocent preborn child.

Plainly put, from the perspective of the medical sciences, human dignity, and the highest of human vocations, abortion is clearly and abhorrently evil. How is it possible, then, that so many reasonable and educated people can accept this atrocity? How can so many people be so complacent in the face of such evil?

> "Any country that accepts abortion, is
> not teaching its people to love, but to use
> any violence to get what it wants."
>
> —Saint Teresa of Calcutta

Radical Autonomy and an Absolutized Freedom

In a normal and just society, the evil of abortion would readily be seen, called out, and denounced. The exception, however, is that other voices and influences have usurped the public narrative. In particular, the predominant notions of radical autonomy and absolutized freedom lend themselves to an arena where preborn life is relativized and minimalized. Therefore, we must unmask these two cultural presumptions.

First, let's address radical autonomy. This is an inflation of human autonomy, which is a good thing when properly understood and lived well.

Autonomy is our self-will. In philosophical terms, autonomy is our self-possession. It is the power we have over ourselves. It empowers us to act and to pursue a good way of life. Properly understood, autonomy is contingent upon others. It is about a tempered independence. It interacts within a vast network of interpersonal relationships, which includes God, spouse and family, colleagues, and community interactions. Autonomy has rights because it has responsibilities. Autonomy consists of duties as much as it consists of personal powers and privileges.

When autonomy is radicalized, it ignores its duties, denies its dependency on anything or anyone, and distances itself from God, family, and other relationships. In this state, autonomy pretends to be a "sovereign self." It becomes narcissistic, self-centered, and aggressive in defense of its imagined independence. Such a wayward notion of autonomy is reflected in such chants as "My body, my choice!"

A false notion of autonomy depends on an absolutized freedom. The two always accompany each other. An absolutized freedom is reflected in such statements as "It's a woman's right to have an abortion." Such an extreme view sees freedom as the only good. It eclipses every other aspect of reality, whether it's in the realm of science, human dignity, or human rights. When this subjugation happens, freedom ceases to be true freedom and instead becomes licentiousness, a moral theory in which we are governed by our own personal whims and wishes. Such a fallen freedom justifies anything that a person wants to do, including the taking of life.

Properly understood, freedom is not the power to do whatever we want. Freedom is the power to do what is right and good. And, similar to autonomy, freedom only has rights because it has responsibilities. Freedom serves life, human dignity, and the common good. If freedom betrays these goods, then it ceases to be freedom. Instead, it becomes a disguised self-totalitarianism.

These deviant notions of autonomy and freedom create a culture in which abortion seems justifiable. Such a culture even argues that abortion is "morally obligatory" in any case in which a woman's radical autonomy or absolutized freedom are threatened. This state of affairs shows the deadly consequences of these views when they're applied to life, especially that of the most vulnerable and weak.

Once unmasked and properly understood, autonomy and freedom are the first two witnesses to the beauty and dignity of every human life and of the utter abhorrence of abortion. It is for this reason that dark forces wish to manipulate and redefine these realities.

What is our understanding of our autonomy? Do we live as if we are a sovereign self, or do we accept and actively live within a vast network of relationships? Do we understand the duties and responsibilities that come with our freedom?

> "It is a poverty to decide that a child must
> die so that you may live as you wish."
> —Saint Teresa of Calcutta

Moral Truth and Preeminence

Within the moral teachings of the Church, there is a certain ordering, or hierarchy, of truths. Such an order does not mean that one issue is more true or less true than any other but rather that the absoluteness of one is greater than the others in terms of how it is lived and applied to our lives and to society. For example, as we will see in future chapters, there is a lot of room given for prudential judgments on immigration or care of the environment, whereas such room for discernment is not present when it comes to abortion.

This difference between moral issues exists for three primary reasons: the clarity of the issue, its grave effects to moral goodness, and the possibility of several other virtues accompanying—or broadening—the issue at hand. And so, immigration must account for many diverse factors in order to reach a level of moral goodness. The taking of a preborn life does not require any discussion because it is always wrong. Abortion, therefore, is clearly and unequivocally denounced by the Church. Any attempt to relativize it with another "life issue" is a singular offense to human dignity and to the hierarchy of moral truths.

It is poor theology, or wayward social policy, to attempt to equate the clear evil of abortion with the prudential nature of other social questions. Such exaggerated thought is oftentimes heard among liberal theologians; namely, "Yes, abortion is terrible, but so are our immigration laws." A faulty comparison such as this is the equivalent of theological bread and circuses.

In ancient Rome, whenever an emperor was found unfavorable, because of a military defeat, gross public immorality, or over taxation, the emperor would simply order that bread be thrown to the commoners and the entertainment in the circuses be increased. Regrettably, these basic measures would distract and satisfy the masses, and the emperor would bear no accountability for his poor skills in thought, government, or fiscal management. It worked every time.

Many liberal theologians today rely on the busyness, the emotive reactions, and the flawed catechetical formation of the people in the pews. As such, they create catchy phrases or illogical comparisons and pass them off as wisdom and counsel. They offend the minds and consciences of believers and people of goodwill by throwing such intellectual bread and circuses into the mix, and then they enjoy their influence, popularity, and supposed status as experts on social issues. Such an approach is a violation of the truth and of the sacred trust given to the ordained and to those trained in theology.

As summarized in the quote at the end of this section from Pope Saint John Paul II, the Church sees all other human rights and life issues as dependent upon and flowing from the proper defense and explanation of life at its most vulnerable and initial stage. Abortion, therefore, is properly regarded as the *preeminent* life issue. As such, it surpasses all other life and social issues. Abortion cannot be compared or relativized to any other moral question or concern. It is preeminent. It is first and foremost in all moral discernment on life and social issues.

Ask yourself: Do I have a clear understanding of the difference between moral issues? Do I recognize that some moral issues are clearer than others? Do I accept and realize the preeminence of abortion over all other life and social issues?

"The inviolability of the person which is a reflection of the absolute inviolability of God, finds its primary and fundamental expression in the inviolability of human life. Above all, the common outcry, which is justly made on behalf of human rights—for example, the right to health, to home, to work, to family, to culture—is false and illusory if the right to life, the most basic and fundamental right and the condition for all other personal rights, is not defended with maximum determination."

—Pope Saint John Paul II, apostolic exhortation
Christifidelis Laici, no. 38

"Seamless Garment"

In mentioning theological bread and circuses, the popular concept of "the seamless garment" needs to be addressed. Regrettably, the concept now has several different definitions, and so a broad evaluation cannot be given. Instead, a summary of the classical seamless garment theory will be given, as well as a review of a morally-sound seamless garment theory. (Although, in full honesty, the term should be avoided because of its historical errors in moral theology.)

The classical seamless garment theory was promoted by the late Cardinal Joseph Bernardin, along with many other moral theologians and ethical philosophers. The theory argues for a consistent life ethic, which means that no issue (such as abortion) has a preeminence. Rather, all issues of life are equal and must be mutually argued in defense of the totality of life and its dignity. Such a view dismisses the notion of a hierarchy of moral truths, the difference between intrinsic evil and prudential judgment among moral issues, and, obviously, the preeminence of abortion among life and social issues. In many respects, therefore, by its own summary, the classical seamless garment theory is contrary to the Catholic moral tradition. In addition, the catchy name "seamless garment," which is a reference to the garment of the Lord Jesus on Mount Calvary (see Jn 19:23), is a well-disguised version of what moral theology calls *proportionalism*, a popular moral approach among secular Westerners.

The concept of proportionalism argues that all moral issues are on an equal plane. There are no intrinsically evil acts, per se. All moral acts must be evaluated ("proportioned") only in relation to a specific situation. In such a case, issues are weighed according to their perceived results. The interior nature of a moral act is not considered. Circumstances and intention, combined with worldly results, are the only standards. If moral issues or principles conflict, then the one that bears the most results must be chosen. In such a concept, abortion could be justified (or even morally obligatory) in certain cases. This is a grossly misguided concept that ultimately denies good and evil. It is an exaggerated principle of double effect and utilitarianism. In a culture that values results, even at the expense of moral truth, proportionalism will always be popular and will always find willing ears, especially among believers and theologians seeking to appease the world.

As mentioned, there are now "spin off" theories that also go under the title of seamless garment. One such theory argues for the consistent life ethic but acknowledges a hierarchy of

truth. This theory confirms that life is the first and fundamental right above all other moral and social issues, and that
abortion is the preeminent issue, but it also states that other
issues need to be addressed as well (even if in a subordinate
way). Such a revisionist version of the seamless garment is
sound in its moral theology but still dirtied by its association
with the classical (and errant) seamless garment theory.

With these clarifications noted, we need to ask some pressing
questions of ourselves: Do we see the seductive power of proportionalism? Are we watchful of our desire for worldly results
or acceptance, even above moral truth? Are we able to disman-
tle proportionalism and defend human life in the womb?

"Among all the crimes which can be committed
against life, procured abortion has characteristics
making it particularly serious and deplorable."

—Pope Saint John Paul II, encyclical letter
Evangelium Vitae, no. 58

FORTITUDE IN THE TRENCHES

As we see the many intellectual and cultural threats to human
life, we can begin to grasp the high importance of the virtue of
fortitude. Christian believers and people of goodwill are summoned to know the arguments that promote or that make abortion sound less abhorrent. They must know how to respond to
them and be willing to always speak the truth in love.

People of faith and goodwill are naturally people of life.
Now, more than ever before, they are also called to be a people of fortitude. Good people must stand up and speak the
truth. They must unapologetically defend life.

KEY TAKEAWAYS

As a quick reference, here are the key takeaways of the teachings on abortion and preeminence:

- Abortion is a direct attack on life in its initial and most vulnerable stage. As such, it is an intrinsically evil act. No circumstance or intention can justify it.
- Radical autonomy and absolutized freedom create a cultural context in which abortion falsely appears justifiable.
- Intrinsically evil acts (such as abortion) are different from moral questions that call for prudential judgments (such as immigration or care for the environment).
- It is an error to argue that prudential moral decisions are equal to intrinsically evil acts.
- There is a hierarchy of moral truths in theology.
- Abortion is the preeminent issue among life and social issues since it deals with life at its initial and most vulnerable stage.
- The classical "seamless garment" theory is a disguised version of proportionalism, which argues that all moral issues are equal and that the goodness of an act is proportionate to its results.
- Proportionalism is popular in utilitarian cultures. It denies moral truth.
- Fortitude is the virtue by which people stand up for what is right and true.

Going to the Mountain

Having presented our arguments, and always seeking to speak the truth in love, we now retreat and go to the mountain for prayer, spiritual rejuvenation, and supplication.

PRAYER

Heavenly Father,
You are the Lord and the Giver of Life,
You protect the innocent,
And guard the vulnerable.
You claim each child as Your own.
You are the Guardian of the Womb,
And the Protector of the Innocent.
You call Your people to defend life
And to cherish it.
We ask Your blessings
As we seek to fulfill this mandate.
Give us Your strength
As we seek to do Your will.
Through Christ Our Lord.
Amen.

EXAMINATION OF CONSCIENCE

The following questions are given as help to examine our consciences on the issue of abortion and preeminence:

- Do I cherish all life as a gift from God?
- Do I place conditions on the dignity of human life based on its faculties and powers?

- Do I falsely proportion the other life issues and neglect the preeminence of abortion?
- Do I think I'm enlightened and above such questions as abortion?
- Do I have a holistic understanding of autonomy and freedom?
- Have I supported groups that fund abortion or voted for pro-abortion candidates?
- Do I offer time and/or financial support to pro-life efforts?
- Do I offer a warm welcome and support to unwed mothers?
- Do I pray for the preborn and their mothers?
- Am I worried about the opinion of others, remaining silent about my support of life and opposition to abortion?

Based on the insights of this examination of conscience, you're encouraged to go make a good confession.

After reviewing this social issue, recommit yourself to the Lordship of Jesus Christ and ask for the intercession of your guardian angel.

"Suscipe" Prayer

Take, Lord, and receive all my liberty,
my memory, my understanding,
and my entire will,
All I have and call my own.

You have given all to me.
To You, Lord, I return it.

Everything is Yours; do with it what You will.
Give me only Your love and Your grace,
that is enough for me.
Amen.

Guardian Angel Prayer

Angel of God,
My guardian dear,
To whom God's love
Commits me here.
Ever this day,
Be at my side,
To light and guard
To rule and guide.
Amen.

Added Devotional

A suggested devotional: Pray the Joyful Mysteries of the Rosary, especially the first mystery: the annunciation of the angel Gabriel to Our Lady and the incarnation of the Eternal Son in the womb of His mother. In your prayer, reflect on human dignity, the preborn Christ in the womb of His mother, and the humanity of all preborn children.

A suggested devotional: Pray the Stations of the Cross, especially the eighth station: Jesus meets the women of Jerusalem. In your prayer, pray for the women who have chosen abortion and for the repose of their innocent children.

Suggested saintly intercessors: Saint (Mother) Teresa of Calcutta, Saint Gianna Beretta Molla, Saints Louis and Zelie

Martin, Saint Gerard Majella, Saint Raymond Nonnatus, Saint Brigid of Ireland, and Saint Philomena. Also suggested is now Venerable Jerome Lejeune.

"The Lord has loved me so much: we must love everyone. . . . We must be compassionate!"

—Saint Josephine Bakhita

"We must love our neighbor as being made in the image of God and as an object of his love."

—Saint Vincent de Paul

Citations from the Catechism of the Catholic Church

Fortitude: 1808
Human Dignity: 1700–15, 1929–30
Natural Rights: 1928–48
Preeminence: 90, 2270, 2273
Freedom: 1730–38, 1743–45
Evil Acts: 1755–56, 1761
Abortion: 2258–2330

CHAPTER 2

Immigration and Prudence

"For I was hungry and you gave me food, I was thirsty and you gave me drink, I was a stranger and you welcomed me."

—Matthew 25:35

Building a Foundation

Before we present the issue of immigration, it's critical that we have a sense of virtue and some guiding principles from the Church's social doctrine.

VIRTUE: *PRUDENCE*
(SEE *CCC* 1806)

Prudence is a high moral virtue. It helps a person discern what is good in different circumstances and states of affairs. It empowers a person to process and choose the right means to achieve what is recognized as good. Prudence is our human reason acting in a good way to achieve a recognized good. It is not to be confused with compromise, fear, pretension, self-protection, or duplicity. It is the "charioteer" of all the other virtues. Prudence directs and coordinates the other virtues by setting "rules and measures" over how and when they will be exercised. Prudence guides the judgment of conscience. With the help of prudence, a person applies moral principles to a particular situation, seeking to do good and avoid evil.

Principle: *Solidarity*
(see *CCC* 1939–42)

Solidarity is the principle by which human beings are called to friendship and social charity with one another. It is "a direct demand of human and Christian brotherhood." It is the principle by which a person sees all other human beings as his brothers or sisters. Solidarity is expressed in spiritual and moral ways but also in material support of others and in compensation for work. Solidarity sees no one as an "outsider." It labors for social tranquility and a more just society for all. It is a foundational principle of society and the common good.

A Second Principle: *Subsidiarity*
(see *CCC* 1883–85)

Subsidiarity is the principle by which human beings are called to express friendship and charity in a series of expanding relationships. It seeks out the most appropriate level for any given care or support, and seeks to be as close as possible to human relationships while avoiding excessive interventions by higher relationships that can threaten personal freedom and initiative. As such, subsidiarity seeks to prevent a community of a higher order interfering in the internal life of a community of a lower order. Subsidiarity never deprives any community of its proper functions. It calls for support and coordination between higher and lower communities only when needed. It is a foundational principle of society and the common good.

Taking Our Stand

Since we have the assistance of virtue, and of some principles from the Church's social doctrine, we are now ready to dive into the question of immigration and prudence.

INTRINSIC VERSUS PRUDENTIAL

As we begin our discussion on immigration, the hierarchy of moral truths has to be indicated and asserted. As you might recall from the previous chapter, there are moral issues that have an intrinsic identity, which means they are *always* deemed morally evil. No intentions or circumstances can ever make them acceptable. Because of this clear moral designation, they hold higher positions in the hierarchy of truths.

Flowing from the moral issues with intrinsic worth, we have the moral issues that require prudential judgment. These issues are serious and pressing, but they do not contain an intrinsic identity and, therefore, can be applied or exercised in different ways. The virtue of prudence is essential, and people of goodwill are free to disagree as to when or how such issues are approached.

Immigration is one of the prudential issues. It is a social issue that does not contain an intrinsic identity. As such, we must take into account the array of factors involved in specific situations, as well as the circumstances and intentions of the groups who are involved in a particular time and place, in order to discern and compose a moral system of laws and policies regarding immigration. And even when such laws and policies are set, people are free to disagree, point out areas of weakness, and work to revise and reform them.

The above distinction between intrinsic moral issues and prudential moral issues is essential for the person who wants to understand social issues and the moral teaching of the Church's social doctrine. Regrettably, there are some liberal theologians who purposely rely on a lack of knowledge among believers and create faulty comparisons that are not in harmony with the important distinction between intrinsic and prudential issues.

With this clarification, a believer is now able to dissect and address the errant statement "Yes, abortion is bad, but so are our immigration laws." The first statement can be made definitively, while the second statement requires discernment and the exercise of prudence.

In our moral discernment, do we make this necessary distinction between intrinsic and prudential issues? Are we willing to do the hard work of exercising prudence in the social arena? Do we understand the importance of having immigration laws and policies that respect both justice and generosity?

"In the case of the positive moral precepts, prudence always has the task of verifying that they apply in a specific situation, for example, in view of other duties which may be more important or urgent. But the negative moral precepts, those prohibiting certain concrete actions or kinds of behavior as intrinsically evil, do not allow for any legitimate exception. They do not leave room, in any morally acceptable way, for the 'creativity' of any contrary determination whatsoever. Once the moral species of an action prohibited by a universal rule is concretely recognized, the only morally good act is that of obeying the moral law and of refraining from the action which it forbids."

—Pope Saint John Paul II, encyclical letter
Veritatis Splendor, no. 67

The Balance Between Two Principles

Since we've indicated that immigration is a moral issue that requires prudence, let's dive in and put this great virtue to work. When we approach immigration, we need to apply both solidarity and subsidiarity, which are two diverse but complementary principles of our social doctrine.

Solidarity teaches us that we are called to be brothers or sisters to all men and women, that we must have an open heart, a loving spirit, and generosity towards everyone we meet. Solidarity emphasizes the natural bond among all human beings as the children of God and members of the human family.

It cannot, however, stand alone. Left to its own devices, and taken to extremes, solidarity leads a society to socialism. Socialism violates our natural rights to personal dignity and identity, to the private ownership of property and capital, and to religious expression. *Solidarity needs subsidiarity*.

Subsidiarity teaches us that our love, commitment, and generosity towards others consist of a series of ever-expanding circles of relationships. Subsidiarity begins in our spiritual hearts, where we encounter God and possess ourselves. Such an autonomy is the foundation of every other relationship we have, since we love others as we love ourselves. This autonomy, however, is not sovereign. It interacts with and is dependent upon others. For many, this is a spouse and family. The possession of one's spiritual heart broadens and includes marriage and children. Subsidiarity guides this movement. From the family, we have intermediate groups, such as houses of worship, neighborhoods, workplaces, and civic organizations. Only then do we reach society, states, countries, and, finally, the world as a "community of nations."

Solidarity guards the lower communities from any encroachment by the larger communities. Solidarity reminds us to pay attention first to the group that is most immediate to us and then to move to the others.

Left to its own devices, and taken to extremes, subsidiarity leads a society to fascism. Fascism violates our natural rights to assemble with others and form families, to have free ideas and freedom of speech, and to exercise self-determination.

Subsidiarity needs solidarity, and vice versa. Subsidiarity reminds us, "Charity begins at home," and solidarity reminds us, "But it doesn't stop there." The two principles are needed for a morally healthy and vibrant society. They are both key to our discernment and prudential judgments on immigration.

As we weigh in on the issue of immigration, we must apply both subsidiarity and solidarity. We must balance the well-being of one group of people seeking a better life with the effects immigrants may have on the society who welcomes them. Neither group has a monopoly on the moral discernment. Both groups, and their legitimate hopes and concerns, must be considered if a morally sound decision is to be made that honors both moral truth and human dignity. Again, prudence helps us find this balance.

Do we realize the high importance of prudence? Why is prudence so important in the broad areas of our social doctrine? Where else can we exercise this virtue in our lives?

"Virtue without prudence is not virtue at all. We should often pray to the Holy Spirit for this grace of prudence. Prudence consists in discretion, rational reflection, and courageous resolution. The final decision is always up to us."

—Saint Faustina

"Maybe They Did . . ."

Some time ago, I was speaking with a Christian social worker who had a heart for the poor, forgotten, and displaced. The work of this holy woman spoke for itself as she poured herself out in selfless service to others. In our conversation, the social worker expressed her frustration over other Christian believers who appeared not to care about those in need. In particular, she was upset about the diversity of views on immigration and the care of the displaced. She believed in a broad and open approach to immigration. In her anger, she said to me, "I just wish that those with strict views on immigration would pray. I wish they would spend some time in conversation with the Lord. Don't they understand that lives are at stake?"

I waited and let this love-filled advocate voice her frustrations and concerns. After a little while, I finally responded. "Well, maybe they did pray. Maybe they took other factors into account and have different views for good reasons."

"What do you mean, Father? Don't you realize that lives are at stake?"

"Yes," I responded, "lives are at stake *on both sides of the issue*. Maybe those with stricter views on immigration are taking into account the well-being of the people here, such as the working class or those on government assistance."

Needless to say, the conversation did not end well. As much as I tried to show that good people can have different views on immigration, and that good people can have strict views on immigration for good reasons, it wasn't well received. The simple point that someone could disagree with our views and not be a monster who is obsessed with greed or self-interest wasn't readily accepted. The idea that others have discerned the issue and seen things from a different perspective was considered a betrayal rather than an opportunity for dialogue, learning, and a better solution founded upon prudence and compromise.

In our processing of prudential moral issues, we all have to be very careful about ideology or a narrow-minded way of thinking. Ideology cancels out dialogue and makes personal views tyrannical. It doesn't allow for a legitimate diversity of views and sees no possibility of each side cooperating together and learning from each other.

Prudence dismisses one-sided thinking. It relies on an unsparing exchange of ideas, perspectives, and possible solutions. It calls for kindness, goodwill, and the benefit of the doubt toward others who are trying to figure out a social issue and who might disagree with us on the best possible solution.

In our moral reflection on prudential issues, do we assume the best of others, especially those that disagree with us? Do we attempt to see issues from the perspective of others? Are we patient in explaining our own views, or do we jump to judgments about others?

"Prudence has eyes, and love has legs. Love, which
has legs, would like to run to God, but its impulse
is blind, and it would often stumble if it were not
for the eyes of prudence. Prudence, when it sees
that love should be restrained, offers its eyes."

—Saint Pio of Pietrelcina

Generosity and Capacity

In our prudential discernment on immigration, we are
assisted by the moral teachings of the Church. In particular,
exercising both solidarity and subsidiarity, the Church calls
for generosity in welcoming immigrants, while also calling
for a consideration of the true capacity of a prospective host
country to welcome them.

The Church directs the more prosperous nations of the
world to be generous in their immigration laws and policies.
The Church even speaks in terms of a moral "obligation" in
welcoming the foreigner and respecting the natural rights of
others, especially those seeking asylum or protection. Such
a summons must be taken seriously, as a nation's wealth is a
blessing that must be responsibly shared with others.

All nations are edified and enriched by immigrants. They
bring a diversity of views that enhance a nation's moral and cultural fabric. As such, immigrants should be readily and generously received and accepted by the various nations of the world.

"The more prosperous nations are obliged, to the extent
they are able, to welcome the foreigner in search of the
security and the means of livelihood which he cannot
find in his country of origin. Public authorities should

see to it that the natural right is respected that places a
guest under the protection of those who receive him."

—*Catechism of the Catholic Church*, no. 2241

The Church, however, notes that such generosity of nations
must be according to "the extent they are able." The Church's
wisdom allows for a certain prudential discernment by a
society and its political leadership. In essence, the generosity
of a nation must flow out of the initial care and well-being
of the current citizens of the nation. The Church further
confirms this authority of political leadership by insisting
that any of its decisions must be done "for the sake of the
common good for which they are responsible."

By extension, while the Church acknowledges the natural right of people to immigrate, especially in their efforts
to provide for basic human needs for themselves and their
loved ones, the Church also teaches that political leadership
can impose various juridical conditions upon a person's natural right to immigrate into their nation. Such juridical conditions are an exercise of justice to the common good under
the care and authority of the deciding political leadership.

"Political authorities, for the sake of the common good
for which they are responsible, may make the exercise
of the right to immigrate subject to various juridical
conditions, especially with regard to the immigrants'
duties toward their country of adoption. Immigrants
are obliged to respect with gratitude the material and
spiritual heritage of the country that receives them, to
obey its laws and to assist in carrying civic burdens."

—*Catechism of the Catholic Church*, no. 2241

These aspects of the Church's teachings show the delicate balance between generosity and genuine capacity, between care of immigrants and attention to the citizens of a country, between natural rights and their exercise, and, ultimately, between solidarity and subsidiarity.

The task is to allow these different aspects to complement, mold, and shape each other into a fair and just body of laws and policies for both the immigrant community and the current citizenry of a nation. Such a task is never easy. It is rarely perfect in our fallen world, which is marked by fluidity and uncertainty.

Do we realize the complexity of the issue of immigration? Do we reflect on the different aspects of the issue? Are we open to the opinions and thoughts of others?

Illegal Immigration and Civic Obedience

While often purposely merged together by some social commentators, there is a clear difference between legal and illegal immigration. Political leadership, exercising the authority entrusted to it, prudentially evaluates, concludes, and promulgates the laws and policies on immigration. These laws are within the virtue of justice and are morally binding on people. Christians are obliged to obey the just laws of respective nations. Violations of just laws are rightly followed by punitive intervention by law enforcement agencies of the nations involved.

"Those subject to authority should regard those in authority as representatives of God, who has made them stewards of his gifts. . . . Their loyal collaboration

includes the right, and at times the duty, to voice their
just criticisms of that which seems harmful to the
dignity of persons and to the good of the community."

—*Catechism of the Catholic Church*, no. 2238

With that said, the Church is adamant that all people,
regardless of their legal status, must have their human dignity respected. As such, they deserve a level of care that
provides for their basic human needs, such as food, urgent
medical care, and shelter.

As a moral teacher, the Church also calls on the integrity of the family to be acknowledged and preserved during
immigration processes and law enforcement interventions.
Of course, children must be protected and groups claiming
to be families need to be authenticated.

Even as the Church supports the rights of nations to create and enforce immigration laws, she calls on world leaders and societies to avoid nurturing any fear of foreigners.
She further denounces any and all forms of discrimination,
injustice, or violence against immigrants, legal or illegal.

"The Church acts in continuity with Christ's mission.
In particular, she asks herself how to meet the needs,
while respecting the law, of those persons who are
not allowed to remain in a national territory."

—Pope Saint John Paul II, *Annual Message for
World Immigration Day*, 1996

The Church calls on the nations of the world to address the reasons for immigration and to propose solutions to the economic,
political, and social causes that force widespread immigration

from certain countries or regions of the world. And so, the balance between the support of just laws and the care of immigrants are equally supported and insisted upon by the Church.

Ask yourself: Do I grasp the difference between legal and illegal immigration? Do I understand the balance between supporting just laws on immigration and the rights of illegal immigrants to basic care and fair treatment?

Harming a Suppliant

While prudence and justice might be applied to immigration policies and laws, there can never be willful or socially approved mistreatment or misrepresentation of immigrants. In the Church's tradition, any harm or brutalization of immigrants is included in a small set of grave sins "that cry to heaven for vengeance."

The cry of an oppressed people, or of a foreigner, is heard by God as the cry of a suppliant—namely, a person who has no other protection or resources other than God's providence. Such mistreatment, however, should not be falsely applied to just laws that prudentially limit immigration, as well as efforts to enforce such laws.

Ask yourself: Do I realize the grave sin of hurting or harming a suppliant? Do I understand the difference between mistreatment and a just enforcement of prudential laws?

"The catechetical tradition also recalls that there are *sins that cry to heaven*: the blood of Abel, the sin of the Sodomites, the cry of the people oppressed in Egypt, the cry of the foreigner, the widow, and the orphan, injustice to the wage earner."

—*Catechism of the Catholic Church*, no. 1867

Prudence in the Trenches

As we see the complexity of the issue of immigration, we realize the need and importance of the virtue of prudence. Christian believers and people of goodwill are called to know the multifaceted and diverse aspects relating to immigration in our world. As such, they must apply justice and right judgment to their deliberations and discernment.

People of faith and goodwill naturally welcome others and embrace those who are different from them. Such an openness needs the help of prudence, which assesses the best possible good in a given state of affairs. Good people must be welcoming but also prudential.

Key Takeaways

As a quick reference, here are the key takeaways of the teachings on immigration and prudence:

- There is a precise distinction between moral issues that have an intrinsic identity, such as abortion, and those that require prudential discernment, such as immigration.
- Immigration is a moral good. It allows for the flourishing and enrichment of both the immigrants and the society that welcomes them.
- Immigration requires the exercise of prudence in balancing the principles of solidarity and subsidiarity.
- Prosperous nations are called to be generous in welcoming immigrants.
- The generosity of nations must be balanced within the true capabilities—"as they are able"—of the respective nation.

- Political authority must make its decisions and act according to what is beneficial to the society entrusted to its care.
- Immigration laws and policies will never be perfect. They are fluid and require reform. The best reform is brought about by an openness to different opinions and solutions.
- The Church calls for a respect and obedience to just immigration laws promulgated by political leadership.
- The dignity of illegal immigrants must be honored, and their basic human needs must be provided for during law enforcement interventions.

Going to the Mountain

Having presented our arguments, and always seeking to speak the truth in love, we now retreat and go to the mountain for prayer, spiritual rejuvenation, and supplication.

Prayer

Heavenly Father,
You are the Lord of all.
You have formed the boundaries of every nation,
You have blessed all peoples,
You have called Your children to love justice and peace.
Help us as we seek to do what is right.
Direct the laws and policies of our nation.
Help us to balance an openness of heart with a
realization of our limits.
Strengthen us to be generous.

Enlighten us to be prudential.
Protect those in need.
Guide those who are seeking a better place for
themselves and their families.
Allow goodness to triumph
as we seek to do Your will.
Through Christ Our Lord.
Amen.

EXAMINATION OF CONSCIENCE

The following questions are given as help to examine our consciences on the issue of immigration and prudence.

- Do I have a welcoming spirit and accept those who are different from me?
- Have I sought to actively help those in need?
- Do I consider the plight of immigrants, who oftentimes simply desire to provide for the basic human needs of themselves and their families?
- Do I have a generous heart? Am I willing to share from my material means?
- Do I exercise the virtue of prudence?
- Do I struggle with xenophobia, racism, or any other form of discrimination?
- Do I understand the complexity of immigration and seek to understand the opinions of others?
- Do I obey just laws when employing or seeking the services of others?
- Have I communicated my opinions on immigration to political leadership?

- Are my views on immigration based on sound and morally good arguments?

Based on the insights of this examination of conscience, you're encouraged to go and make a good confession.

After reviewing this social issue, recommit yourself to the Lordship of Jesus Christ, and ask for the intercession of your guardian angel.

"Suscipe" Prayer

Take, Lord, and receive all my liberty,
my memory, my understanding,
and my entire will,
All I have and call my own.

You have given all to me.
To You, Lord, I return it.

Everything is Yours; do with it what You will.
Give me only Your love and Your grace,
that is enough for me.
Amen.

Guardian Angel Prayer

Angel of God,
My guardian dear,
To whom God's love
Commits me here.
Ever this day,
Be at my side,
To light and guard

To rule and guide.
Amen.

ADDED DEVOTIONAL

A suggested devotional: Pray the Joyful Mysteries of the Rosary, especially the second mystery: the visitation of the Blessed Mother to her kinswoman Elizabeth. In your prayer, focus on human dignity, the beautiful charity and graciousness exchanged between these two holy women, and the kindness and welcoming spirit that we are called to offer all people.

A suggested devotional: Pray the Stations of the Cross, especially the Tenth Station: Jesus is stripped of His garments. In your prayer, pray for just immigration laws and for the care of those who have no legal status and are trying to support their families.

Suggested saintly intercessors: Saint Joseph, Saint Francis Xavier Cabrini, and Saint Toribio Romo Gonzalez. Also suggested is Blessed John Baptist Scalabrini.

"For the Christian, every human being is a 'neighbor' to be loved. He should not ask himself whom he should love, because to ask 'who is my neighbor?' is already to set limits and conditions."

—Pope Saint John Paul II

"Don't judge without having heard both sides. Even persons who think themselves virtuous very easily forget this elementary rule of prudence."

—Saint Josemaria Escriva

CITATIONS FROM THE
CATECHISM OF THE CATHOLIC CHURCH

Prudence: 1806
Human Dignity: 1700–15, 1929–30
Evil Acts: 1755–56, 1761
Political Authority: 2234–40
Solidarity: 1939–42
Subsidiarity: 1883–85
Immigration: 2241

CHAPTER 3

The Environment and Stewardship

*"When I look at your heavens, the work of your fingers, the moon
and the stars that you have established; what is man that you are
mindful of him, and the son of man that you care for him? Yet
you have made him little less than God, and crowned him with
glory and honor. You have given him dominion over the works
of your hands; you have put all things under his feet, all sheep
and oxen, and also the beasts of the field, the birds of the air, and
the fish of the sea, whatever passes along the paths of the seas."*

—*Psalm 8:3–8*

Building a Foundation

Before we present the issue of the environment, it's critical
that we have a sense of virtue and some guiding principles
from the Church's social doctrine.

VIRTUE: *HOPE*
(SEE *CCC* 1817–21, 1843)

Hope is one of the highest virtues of the Christian way of
life. It has a supernatural expression since it helps us to hope
in God. Hope is expressed in our resolution to place the
kingdom of God above all things. It teaches us not to rely

on our own strength or the resources of this world but to depend solely upon the grace of God. Hope purifies our actions such that they work toward our salvation in Jesus Christ. Hope preserves us from selfishness and helps us to yearn for heaven.

PRINCIPLE: *HUMAN DIGNITY*
(SEE *CCC* 27, 306–8, 356–57, 364, 369, 872, 1004, 1700–15, 1730, 1929–30, 1934, 2158, 2203, 2334)

The principle of human dignity asserts that every human person is made in the image of God. Human dignity shows that every human being is a *someone*, not a *something*. Thus, every human person has the power to act on their own and is capable of self-knowledge, of self-possession, and of freely giving himself and entering into communion with other persons. Human dignity upholds that the human person is an intelligent and free cause who, by knowledge and love, can share in God's own life. While such dignity can regrettably be eclipsed and offended, it cannot be taken away by any created entity, including the person himself.

A SECOND PRINCIPLE: *STEWARDSHIP*
(SEE *CCC* 342–43, 398–400, 2402, 2415–18, 2456–57)

The principle of stewardship reminds humanity that all things have been created by God and operate according to His divine providence. In His plan, God has entrusted human beings with the power to freely share in His providence by entrusting them with the responsibility of subduing the earth and having dominion over it. Such dominion, however, is not absolute. It is guided by moral imperatives and a summons to protect and care for all that God has created.

Taking Our Stand

Since we have the assistance of virtue, and some principles from the Church's social doctrine, we are now ready to dive into the question of the environment and stewardship.

"The Land Is a Part of Us"

My great-grandfather was the brave soul who left Ireland, crossed the Atlantic, and made the United States my family's new home. He came with nothing. He started as a bricklayer and worked his way into the railway industry. He trained dogs on the side, and when his young family needed extra money, he would box at night for quick cash. He was a driven man whose aspirations were to protect and provide for his family.

As a young man, my great-grandfather would never have dreamed of owning a home or possessing his own land. And yet, through hard work and shrewd savings, he eventually bought a home that sat on several acres. My family has passed down stories of how he used to enjoy walking his property in the peace of the early morning. Sometimes he would be gone for hours, just perusing the land and checking on things.

My great-grandfather was affectionately called "the old man." On one occasion, the old man came into his house and called for my father, his grandson. A young Alan J. Kirby was quick to respond and run to meet him at the door.

"Come with me," he said, somewhat grimly.

They left the house, my dad quietly walking alongside the old man. They entered a grove and stopped before a tree with markings on it, etchings of faces, stars, and the initials "AJK."

"Alan, look at what someone did to this tree. Why did they do that? I can't believe someone would mark all over this beautiful tree."

My father was silent.

"This tree is a part of the land, and the land is a part of us. We don't damage it, unless it's to provide for our well-being. And if we have to take a tree down, we replace it. There's nothing more important than the land. Do you understand?"

Young "AJK" swiftly nodded and apologized. Nothing else had to be said. The lesson was learned.

Life went on, and decades later, I was told that story by both my father and my great-grandmother. It was a powerful lesson for my father, and for my generation of the family, but it also points to a broader lesson for all people of goodwill; namely, we must respect the environment because it's a part of us. It's a part of the creation that God has brought into existence and entrusted to our care. We are summoned to respect, prudently use, and honor all that God has made.

In our lives, do we give proper tribute to the environment? Do we realize our call to care for God's creation?

"*The way humanity treats the environment influences the way it treats itself,* and vice versa. This invites contemporary society to a serious review of its life-style, which, in many parts of the world, is prone to hedonism and consumerism. . . . What is needed is an effective shift in mentality which can lead to the adoption of *new life-styles*."

—Pope Benedict XVI, encyclical letter
Caritas in Veritate, no. 51

GOD AS CREATOR AND OUR STEWARDSHIP

As Christian believers, our approach to the environment begins with an acknowledgment of God as the Creator of all things. This simple profession distinguishes us from many environmental activists who see the world as a good *in and of itself*. Yes, as believers, we see creation as "good," even "very good," since it was made, is sustained, and blessed by God, who is All-Good and All-Holy, but it is not our everything. We are obliged to protect and use the environment with prudence because we worship and give thanks to God, not because the environment is some kind of deity. In adoring God, we see an interior order of existence and recognize a call in our hearts to be good stewards of all that God has made and all that He has entrusted to us.

As we use the term *stewardship*, it might be helpful for us to understand what this meant in the ancient world. In older cultures, a steward was a chief servant in the home of his master. The steward supervised the domain, assets, and property of another. He facilitated their use and took charge of their upkeep and maintenance. The steward held the constant responsibility of caring for an estate that belonged to his master and an accountability of having to answer for all of his decisions and actions (or inactions).

In the same way, we are stewards of a world that has been given to us, that we must use for our well-being, but a world, nonetheless, that does not belong to us and for which we will have to answer. And so, the acknowledgment of our stewardship of the earth is the foundation and basis of the entire Christian understanding of our prudential care of the environment.

Do we understand the reasons for our attention to the environment? Do we place God first in all our efforts to protect and care for creation?

"In the beginning God entrusted the earth and its resources to the common stewardship of mankind to take care of them, master them by labor, and enjoy their fruits. The goods of creation are destined for the whole human race."

—*Catechism of the Catholic Church*, no. 2402

ORDER AND HIERARCHY

God created the heavens and the earth. They were brought forth in wisdom. Creation is not an accident or the result of blind chance, nor the mere conclusion of an evolutionary process. Creation comes directly from God's will. He created the world in an ordered, hierarchical, and harmonious way.

God crowned His creation with the human person. Made in God's very image and likeness, the human person possesses both a body and soul and is endowed with the power to share in God's own life. As such, the human person is not equal to any other material creation. Animals, plants, and the environment have worth and should be valued, but they are subordinate to the human person and exist in service to humanity's well-being.

As the central masterpiece of creation, humanity participates in the wisdom and goodness of the Creator. He has blessed us with a mastery over our actions (though clouded by sin) so that we can govern ourselves with the help of His grace. He gives us the power to freely share in His providence by giving us the responsibility of subduing the earth and holding dominion over it.

As sharers in God's providence, human persons possess a natural law within their hearts. This law, which can be discerned by our reason, is the original moral sense in which humanity knows right from wrong. It enables us to recognize what is good and true. It distinguishes us from the animals and other aspects of creation.

This internal law is called "natural" not because it speaks of the environment, or a raw nature of irrational beings, but because it speaks to the essence of humanity. It addresses our reason, which participates in God's reason. As such, we can know the order of existence and discern the moral imperatives of goodness and right conduct.

The natural law expresses the dignity of each person and the fundamental rights and duties possessed by every human being. It gives testimony to the hierarchy within existence and speaks of humanity's privileged place in the heart of God's creation.

Do we seek to know God's providential order within creation? Do we recognize the privileged place of the human person in creation? Are we aware of the natural law and our internal ability to know right from wrong?

"Use of the mineral, vegetable, and animal resources of the universe cannot be divorced from respect for moral imperatives. Man's dominion over inanimate and other living beings granted by the Creator is not absolute; it is limited by concern for the quality of life of his

neighbor, including generations to come; it requires
a religious respect for the integrity of creation."

—*Catechism of the Catholic Church*, no. 2415

Gift and Responsibility

God has blessed us with the gift of creation. He is generous
and kind to us, His children, as He provides the world and all
its resources for our care and well-being. As God is gracious,
so He is just. He is good, but He also demands accountability. Whatever God gives to us, He expects that such gifts will
be used responsibly and in accordance with virtue.

This is true of all things, and so it is true of the environment. While the environment is subordinate to us as human
beings, it is a gift from God. We must respect and use it
well and responsibly. As God's children, we are called to see
His majesty and splendor shining through creation. With
this in mind, we must prudentially use creation according
to authentic human needs and with a sincere attention to its
general welfare and security.

As God's children, we are empowered to use the earth,
subdue it, and use its resources to provide for ourselves, our
loved ones, and our society. But we are called to order our
industry in such a way so as to respect the environment as
best as possible, to avoid needless waste or harm to the world
around us, and to seek restoration, replanting, or rebuilding
whenever possible.

First and foremost, we are called to this type of stewardship in praise and thanksgiving of God. We are also called to
this stewardship in service to our fellow man, especially the

poor and those on the periphery of the world, but also for our posterity.

Do we accept our call to a stewardship of the environment? Do we seek to adore God through our care of His creation? Do we value our world today and consider the world that we will pass on to our descendants?

"Christians, in particular, realize that their responsibility within creation and their duty towards nature and the Creator are an essential part of their faith."

—Pope Saint John Paul II,
World Day of Peace Message (1990)

PRUDENTIAL JUDGMENTS

As addressed in previous chapters, there are social issues that require discernment and prudential judgments. In addressing the environment, there are multiple issues that demand reflection and diversity of judgments and opinions in order to reach the best possible solution.

As theologians, scientists, and social policy experts have their prudential judgments, so do senior leaders in the Church. Such judgments, or related theological opinions, are different from magisterial teachings. As believers, magisterial teachings are binding on our consciences (to greater or lesser degree). These are teachings that are connected with the revealed teachings of Jesus Christ and are within the context of faith and morals. We are obliged to give religious assent of intellect and will to these teachings.

While we must adhere to magisterial teachings, we are not obliged to accept prudential judgments or theological opinions.

We are always bound to give respectful attention to any prudential judgment or theological opinion of any person of goodwill. We are particularly enjoined to respect the judgments or opinions of those who hold a sacred office in the Church. We are not, however, compelled to agree with such judgments or opinions. We are free to diverge (and even challenge) the prudential judgments or theological opinions of others, even of those who hold the highest offices in the Church.

Do I know the difference between a magisterial teaching and a prudential judgment? Do I know that I am free to disagree with the prudential judgment of a Church leader?

"Prudence demands humble, disciplined and watchful reason that does not let itself be blinded by prejudices; it does not judge according to desires and passions but rather seeks the truth, even though it may prove uncomfortable. Prudence means searching for the truth and acting in conformity with it. The prudent servant is first and foremost a man of truth and a man of sincere reason."

—Pope Benedict XVI, *Homily at Ordination of New Bishops* (2009)

CLIMATE CHANGE AND CHURCH TEACHING

In the arena of environmental issues, the question of climate change has taken center stage. With regard to this issue, the Church has no official teaching. She cannot. Any views on climate change are in the realm of the natural sciences or theological speculation and would be outside of the competency of magisterial teaching on faith and morals.

Reason helps us see that there has been a change in our climate, as there has always been such changes. And so, there will be perennial and multifaceted debates and arguments by natural and social scientists, as well as speculative theologians, over whether our current climate change is unique in human history, or to what degree the human family is responsible for our current changes in the climate.

If senior clergy choose to enter the debate and discussion, and even to include their opinions in magisterial documents, they are free to do so. But such involvement is classified as prudential judgments or theological opinions, and so we are free to disagree with such views.

Whether there is a man-made cause to climate change or not, our response as Christians is still to be stewards, to care for the earth even as we subdue it, and to seek to show our reverence for God in how we honor His creation.

Have I been attentive to my responsibility as a steward of the earth? Have I sought to care for the earth in my actions and way of life?

"Faced with the widespread destruction of the environment, people everywhere are coming to understand that we cannot continue to use the goods of the earth as we have in the past. The public in general as well as political leaders are concerned about this problem, and experts from a wide range of disciplines are studying its causes. Moreover, a new ecological awareness is beginning to emerge which, rather than being downplayed, ought to be encouraged to develop into concrete programs and initiatives."

—Pope Saint John Paul II,
World Day of Peace Message (1990)

HOPE IN THE TRENCHES

The question of the environment involves a range of issues. Each issue has a chorus of experts with different opinions, judgments, and possible solutions. Christian believers and people of goodwill are called to understand their responsibility to be good stewards of creation. In their care for the earth, however, they should actively exercise the virtue of hope. Hope directs our attention to eternal life. It gives us the goal of our lives and helps us to order everything toward it. This includes our stewardship of the earth. We cannot allow fear, false guilt, or intimidation to overtake us. We are called to do the right thing for the right reason.

People of faith and goodwill naturally care for the earth and the environment. Such a care is enriched and edified by hope. Good people must be attentive to the things of this life, but they must also be raised up and carried by hope.

KEY TAKEAWAYS

As a quick reference, here are the key takeaways of the teachings on the environment and stewardship:

- Moral issues on the environment are prudential issues. They are elevated and assisted by the principle of stewardship and the virtue of hope.
- The principle of stewardship reminds us that God has entrusted humanity with creation and that there will be an accounting for our care of the earth.
- Hope directs the attention of people to eternity. It allows for good things to be done for the right reasons.

- The Christian care for the environment begins with the profession of God as the Creator of all things.
- Creation was brought forth in wisdom. It was made in an ordered, hierarchical, and harmonious way by God.
- The human person is the heart and center of God's creation.
- Human beings have a natural law within their hearts that allow them to participate in the wisdom and reason of God.
- We must exercise our stewardship with the virtues of the children of God.
- Prudential judgments are different from magisterial teachings. Magisterial teachings are in the realm of faith and morals and are binding on the consciences of believers. Prudential judgments are not binding. Believers can disagree (and challenge) such judgments, even if they are held by high churchmen.
- The Church has no official teaching on climate change since the question is outside of the Church's competency of faith and morals.

Going to the Mountain

Having presented our arguments, and always seeking to speak the truth in love, we now retreat and go to the mountain for prayer, spiritual rejuvenation, and supplication.

Prayer

Good and Gracious God,
You are the Father and Creator of all.

We rejoice in the wonders of Your creation!

We celebrate its marvels and beauty!

We thank You, for we are fearfully and wonderfully made.

Open our hearts to care for what You have created.

Inspire in us a spirit of stewardship.

Help us to care for all You have given us.

Guide us to care for our world,

and to subdue it, as You have commanded us.

We praise You! We thank You! We glorify You!

Through Christ Our Lord.

Amen.

EXAMINATION OF CONSCIENCE

The following questions are given as help to examine our consciences on the issue of the environment and stewardship.

- Do I acknowledge God as the Creator of all things?
- Do I pray and praise God for the marvels of His creation?
- Is my stewardship of the earth motivated by fear or by my faith in God?
- Do I try to live and apply the principle of stewardship to my daily life?
- Do I actively look for ways in which I can better care for the world around me?
- Do I seek to understand my unique dignity as a human person?
- Have I kept my conscience clean so as to discern the natural law in my heart?
- Have I attempted to place other created things above

human dignity?

- Do I foster hope and place all the efforts of my life within the context of eternity?
- Am I respectful to the prudential judgments of Church leaders?

Based on the insights of this examination of conscience, you're encouraged to go and make a good confession.

After reviewing this social issue, recommit yourself to the Lordship of Jesus Christ, and ask for the intercession of your guardian angel.

"Suscipe" Prayer

Take, Lord, and receive all my liberty,
my memory, my understanding,
and my entire will,
All I have and call my own.

You have given all to me.
To You, Lord, I return it.

Everything is Yours; do with it what You will.
Give me only Your love and Your grace,
that is enough for me.
Amen.

Guardian Angel Prayer

Angel of God,
My guardian dear,
To whom God's love
Commits me here.

Ever this day,
Be at my side,
To light and guard
To rule and guide.
Amen.

Added Devotional

A suggested devotional: Pray the Glorious Mysteries of the Rosary, especially the first mystery: Our Lord's resurrection from the dead. In your prayer, focus on the glory of creation, the Lord's victory over death and darkness, and the placement of all our actions within a hope for eternal life.

A suggested devotional: Pray the Stations of the Cross, especially the third station: Jesus falls the first time. In your prayer, pray for a greater sense of stewardship among the faithful.

Suggested saintly intercessors: Saint Gertrude of Nivelles, Saint Hubert, Saint Francis of Assisi, and Saint Kateri Tekakwitha.

"I want creation to penetrate you with so much
admiration that wherever you go, the least plant
may bring you clear remembrance of the Creator.
A single plant, a blade of grass, or one speck of
dust is sufficient to occupy all your intelligence in
beholding the art with which it has been made."

—Saint Basil

"God passes through the thicket of the world, and
wherever his glance falls he turns all things to beauty."

—Saint John of the Cross

CITATIONS FROM THE
CATECHISM OF THE CATHOLIC CHURCH

Hope: 1817–21, 1843
Stewardship: 342–43, 398–400, 2402; 2415–18, 2456–57
Creation: 279–324
Human Dignity: 27, 306–8, 356–57, 364, 369, 872, 1004, 1700–15, 1730, 1929–30, 1934, 2158, 2203, 2334
Natural Law: 1954–60

CHAPTER 4

The LGBTQ+ Movement
and Complementarity

*"And Pharisees came up to him and tested him by asking, "Is it
lawful to divorce one's wife for any cause?" He answered, "Have
you not read that he who made them from the beginning made
them male and female, and said, 'For this reason a man shall
leave his father and mother and be joined to his wife, and the
two shall become one'? So they are no longer two but one. What
therefore God has joined together, let not man put asunder."*
                                                —Matthew 19:3–6

Building a Foundation

Before we present the issue of the LGBTQ+ movement, it's
critical that we have a sense of virtue and a guiding principle from the Church's social doctrine.

VIRTUE: LOVE
(SEE CCC 1822–29)

Love is one of the core Christian virtues. It helps us to place
God above all things and to seek the good of our neighbor
above ourselves. Love is not about emotional fulfillment or
about getting our way. Love is self-emptying and focused
on virtue. It is willing to sacrifice and suffer for the sake of

righteousness. Love seeks the genuine good of another. It does not objectify or use another person as a mere means of pleasure, power, advancement, or personal gain. Love includes our enemies, as well as the poor and those who are most forgotten or rejected.

PRINCIPLE: *COMPLEMENTARITY*
(SEE *CCC* 2331–36)

Complementarity is the principle that illustrates the unique and harmonious relationship between man and woman. God created men and women in His own image and placed within them the vocation, capacity, and responsibility of love and communion. Complementarity affects the entire person, body and soul. It demonstrates that our bodies, united to our innermost being, are not accidents that can be manipulated. Our bodies and souls are one. The male person has been formed to match and complete the female person, and vice versa. And so, the nuptial friendship is a particular friendship between one man and one woman for life.

A SECOND PRINCIPLE: *SOLIDARITY*
(SEE *CCC* 1939–42)

Solidarity is the principle by which human beings are called to friendship and social charity with one another. It is "a direct demand of human and Christian brotherhood." It is the principle by which a person sees all other human beings as his brother or sister. Solidarity is expressed in spiritual and moral ways, but also in material support of others and in compensation for work. Solidarity sees no one as an "outsider." It labors for social tranquility and a more just society for all. It is a foundational principle of society and the common good.

Taking Our Stand

Since we have the assistance of virtue, and some principles from the Church's social doctrine, we are now ready to dive into the question of the LGBTQ+ movement and complementarity.

"What Do You See . . ."

Some years back, I attended a local celebration in my hometown and went to the reception afterwards. While I was perusing the buffet line, two women, who were very affectionate with one another, saw my Roman collar and quickly approached me. They pointed and yelled, "You think we're wrong!" I was surprised by the abruptness and simply stated, "Yes, I think you're wrong." They began to fume when I continued, "In looking at your plates, you could have chosen better food from this great buffet!"

In spite of themselves, they laughed, before pressing further. "You think we're wrong. *What do you see* when you look at us?" The women were, of course, referencing their homosexual relationship. They were trying to make a point or pick a fight.

"Here's what I see when I look at the two of you," I said calmly. "I see two children of God, well beloved by Him, who want to share their lives with someone, who want to love and be loved, and have someone alongside them through the joys and sorrows of life. That's the first thing I see when I look at the two of you." They were speechless for a few seconds, until they finally responded, "Well, yes. But you think we're wrong."

I waited a few more seconds and then said, "Yes, I disagree with the way you express yourselves sexually, and we can talk about that. But I know that heart speaks to heart and I understand the importance of having people who love you. Maybe we can talk about that first."

Well, they came and sat with me at a table. Honestly, we didn't talk any more about the big stuff, but we shared a few more laughs and enjoyed the reception together. My point was made and the door was open. I've never heard from these women again, but the beginnings of the message of love were shared and a positive witness was given to the Christian faith.

The story stands on its own, but it also evokes a few questions. We live in a secular society that has completely kowtowed to the LGBTQ+ movement. It affects every part of our social life.

As Christians, what are our teachings on homosexuality and transgenderism? How are we to approach homosexual or transgender people?

"What does love look like? It has the hands to help others.
It has the feet to hasten to the poor and needy. It has
eyes to see misery and want. It has the ears to hear the
sighs and sorrows of men. That is what love looks like."

—Saint Augustine of Hippo

A People of Love

The answer to the question about our teachings on the LGBTQ+ movement is easier to give than the practical question about how we are to approach homosexual or transgender people. In large part, this second question is difficult to answer because we are told that we are homophobic. Simply because we disagree on homosexuality, it is asserted that we are bigoted and discriminatory. It is said, and sometimes yelled at us, that we are closed-minded bullies who hate homosexual and transgender people.

But that's not true. As Christians, we see every human being as a child of God, worthy of respect and love. We advocate no harm or violence to any person. And if someone should attempt to hurt or harm another person—heterosexual, homosexual, or transgender—we Christians are summoned to be the first to defend and protect them and their dignity. As Christians, we are a people of love. It is a love that both speaks the truth and defends all people.

In fact, it is precisely the love that we have for all men and women, and the respect we show to their God-given dignity, that compels us to give witness to the truth and to seek the moral and spiritual well-being of all people. No authentic action of a Christian is born from bigotry or hatred of another person since we are all made in God's image and given the opportunity for salvation in Jesus Christ. And so, the answer to the question about how we are to approach members of the LGBTQ+ movement is rather straightforward. We approach them with the same virtues and openness of heart with which we engage all other people. We see their humanity before their fallenness.

As Christians, we cannot participate in any action, event, or conversation that may give (or be perceived to give) approval, acceptance, or normalization to homosexuality or to transgenderism. Nevertheless, while remaining faithful to moral truth and speaking honestly at all times, we do welcome and accompany any person who desires true friendship and wholesome interaction. If a homosexual or transgender person is intolerant and cannot accept a difference of views on their way of life, then we can charitably distance ourselves from them, praying for them and their conversion.

In our lives, do we approach all people as children of God? Do we speak the truth in love no matter where we are or with whom we are speaking? Even if we are uncomfortable, do we try to befriend those who are outside of a Gospel way of life?

> "[Homosexual persons] must be accepted with respect, compassion, and sensitivity. Every sign of unjust discrimination in their regard should be avoided."
>
> —*Catechism of the Catholic Church*, no. 2358

Fallen Humanity and "Disorders"

We live in a fallen world and possess a fallen human nature. As such, there are numerous disorders that exist within us. Some of the disorders involve our behavior, such as someone who has a disordered appetite for food or telling lies. Meanwhile, some of the other disorders are within our nature and are allowed by God's permissive will, meaning He does not actively desire them but permits them. These would include things such as diabetes or fetal alcohol syndrome.

It is within this context that the Church speaks of the "disorder" of homosexual attraction—namely, when someone has exclusive or predominant desires for sexual acts with people of their same sex. Since man and woman were created with a deep and clearly observable complementarity, any attraction that would break such an ordered, natural union is considered a disordered attraction.

The Church gives no opinion on whether someone is born with such an attraction or whether it is something that is developed by a person's history and life experiences. Either way, the Church points humanity to the natural complementarity of man and woman and rightly identifies homosexual attraction as disordered and calls the person to order their sexuality and live a life of chastity. In giving this teaching, there are some important clarifications that need to be made.

First: Simply because someone believes and/or is adamant that they were "born this way," does not give them moral permission to act on such attractions. As explained, even if people are born with same-sex attractions, such attractions would still be disordered and would not be morally acceptable. God permits many disorders that require sacrifice and life changes so that a person can be healthy and virtuous. For example, a person born with diabetes must change their diet and watch what they eat. Simply because they are born with such a disorder doesn't mean that it should be indulged. Such irresponsible actions would cause harm to their bodies and souls.

Second: The attraction is the disorder, not the person. People with homosexual attractions are born just as good—and fallen—as the rest of humanity. We all bear the image of God within us. People with same-sex attractions are well beloved children of God and must be respected, welcomed, and loved. While we are all fallen, no person is disordered (even if they have one or multiple disorders within them).

There are three other broader clarifications that must be given: the distinction between homosexual orientation and homosexual acts, the path of chastity and holiness of the person who orders their sexuality according to moral truth and goodness, and the importance of friendship. These will be explained in the following sections.

Before addressing those, let's ask ourselves some questions. In our lives, do we recognize the disorders caused by humanity's fallenness? Do we understand the importance of bringing order to the possible disorders in our lives? Do we support people with same-sex attractions who are trying to live virtuous lives?

"Homosexuality refers to relations between men or between women who experience an exclusive or predominant sexual attraction toward persons of the same sex. . . . Its psychological genesis remains largely unexplained."

—*Catechism of the Catholic Church*, no. 2357

HOMOSEXUAL ORIENTATION AND ACTS

Any person who has exclusive or predominant same-sex attractions are said to have a homosexual orientation, which means their sexual desires are oriented toward those of their same sex. While a homosexual orientation is a disorder in and of itself, it is not sinful, and the person who carries such attractions does not bear any moral guilt, so long as they do not intentionally nurture such an orientation. It sometimes happens that a person, especially one of sound faith or goodwill, does not want the attractions and labors and suffers to direct and channel them according to moral truth and goodness.

While a homosexual orientation is not sinful, any homosexual act is gravely sinful. It offends God as Creator, the goodness of creation, and the complementarity of man and woman. Since homosexual acts are not within the realm of natural complementarity, and so do not come from genuine male-female affectivity, they are hedonistic, self-focused, and narcissistic actions. They cause immense harm to the soul of the persons involved in them. Homosexual acts are to be avoided at all costs.

In my moral formation, do I understand the difference between a homosexual orientation and homosexual acts? Do I understand the virtue of the person with a homosexual orientation who seeks to live a godly life? Do I avoid any words, attitudes, or behaviors that are homophobic or offensive to people with such attractions?

"Basing itself on Sacred Scripture, which presents homosexual acts as acts of grave depravity, tradition has always declared that 'homosexual acts are intrinsically disordered.' They are contrary to the natural law. They close the sexual act to the gift of life. They do not proceed from a genuine affective and sexual complementarity. Under no circumstances can they be approved."

—*Catechism of the Catholic Church*, no. 2357

CRY TO HEAVEN FOR VENGEANCE

In identifying the sinfulness of homosexual acts, one further point must be made. There is an attempt by some theologians to include homosexual acts along with fornication and adultery in some type of general list of sexual sins. From such a list, they argue that all of the respective sins are precisely sinful because they're outside of the marital union. While such a presentation might sound good and even "fair," the argument is wrong and the intention is deceptive, especially when it is given by trained theologians.

The argument that homosexual acts are analogous to other sexual sins, however, is mistaken. It subtly works to relativize the severity of homosexual acts. It avoids the deviancy of homosexual acts toward nature. Unlike fornication and adultery (which are indeed gravely sinful), homosexual acts not only violate chastity and the dignity of the marital union but also distinctively reject and manipulate nature. It is for this reason that homosexual acts are included in a rare set of grave sins known as "sins that cry to heaven."

Rather than minimize the sinfulness of homosexual acts, moral truth rightly identifies them as unrivaled in their depravity among sins against chastity since they wage war against nature itself. It is for this reason that homosexual acts are to be seen theologically as possessing their own wayward province among the sins against chastity.

Do we remember to pray for those who are stuck in serious sin? Do we ask for the graces of conversion for those entrenched in a homosexual lifestyle?

"The catechetical tradition also recalls that there are *sins that cry to heaven*: the blood of Abel, the sin

of the Sodomites, the cry of the people oppressed
in Egypt, the cry of the foreigner, the widow, and
the orphan, injustice to the wage earner."

—*Catechism of the Catholic Church*, no. 1867

THE PLACE OF CHASTITY

The person who has a homosexual orientation is called to a
life of chastity. They are given the special mission from the
Lord Jesus to labor to order their sexual desires according
to moral truth and to seek an inner harmony and personal
integration in their spiritual and bodily lives.

"Chastity means the successful integration of
sexuality within the person and thus the inner unity
of man in his bodily and spiritual being. . . . The
virtue of chastity therefore involves the integrity
of the person and the integrality of the gift."

—*Catechism of the Catholic Church*, no. 2337

Unlike the popular attacks on this pastoral direction, such a
call does not doom the person to a life of misery, isolation,
and shame. The reality is quite the opposite. Such a person
is called to live an abundant life by deepening their spiritu-
ality, nurturing healthy friendships, selflessly serving others,
pursuing interests that help the common good, and being an
active member in society and the Church.

"Homosexual persons are called to chastity. By the virtues of self-mastery that teach them inner freedom,
at times by the support of disinterested friendship, by
prayer and sacramental grace, they can and should grad-

ually and resolutely approach Christian perfection."
—*Catechism of the Catholic Church*, no. 2359

The call to chastity is a summons to personal freedom, which blossoms from truth, and to a deeper and purer love for others. People with a homosexual orientation can draw closer to the Lord through their sufferings and joys. They can allow emotional heartache or relational difficulty to become a means by which they can more closely follow and serve the Lord Jesus. Such persons have a particular power in the realm of redemptive suffering, and such a power should not be underestimated by them or anyone else.

In our own struggles with living moral truth, do we remember to pray for others who are also having difficulty? Do we remember to pray for those with homosexual orientations that are living by moral truth?

"The number of men and women who have deep-seated homosexual tendencies is not negligible. This inclination, which is objectively disordered, constitutes for most of them a trial. . . . These persons are called to fulfill God's will in their lives and, if they are Christians, to unite to the sacrifice of the Lord's Cross the difficulties they may encounter from their condition."
—*Catechism of the Catholic Church*, no. 2358

TRANSGENDERISM AND DYSPHORIA

In covering the various aspects of the LGBTQ+ movement, we must give some attention to transgenderism and those who experience gender dysphoria, which is a feeling or experience of disassociation with one's birth gender or physical characteristics relating to it. In general, this is a dissociative condition within the person since they feel one way but are actually another.

In a healthy society, people with such disassociation within themselves would be treated for a mental and emotional disorder. Regrettably, we live in an age in which dualism is the rule of the day. Dualism is the belief that our bodies and souls are radically distinct. In one form of dualism, our bodies are seen as incidental, accidental to the "real" us that dwells somewhere in our interior. It approaches the body as raw material that can be manipulated according to our feelings or subjective experiences. This is the dualism that fuels transgenderism.

Transgenderism is a grave disorder. It is an offense to God, the natural order of creation, and to the proper male and female gender of real life.

Personal maturity has always been viewed as the ability to find harmony between our bodies and souls and to allow our intellect and will (our spiritual soul) to temper and order our feelings and experiences according to reality.

Transgenderism denies all of this. It asserts that God our Creator has made a mistake in the most radical part of our personal identity and that we must "fix it." It argues for the superiority of feelings and experiences over reality.

Our response to those who have such feelings, or who have undergone "sex reassignment" surgery, is one of love and compassion. Regrettably, due to the militant approach of many transgender activists, it can be difficult to welcome and accompany such people. Nevertheless, Christians are called to do their best and seek ways to manifest God's love and acceptance to those in the transgender movement.

The rates of depression and suicide within the transgender movement have not been adequately reported by the various channels of society. When addressed, it is oftentimes asserted that such things occur because of discrimination against transgender people by the broader culture. And yet, such sorrows continue to happen even after someone has "transitioned," and within a society that has now given unbridled acceptance to transitioned people.

It has yet been asked whether such indulgence by society, and sex reassignment surgeries, is a legitimate good for those who experience gender dysphoria. As Christians, we know that gender dysphoria is a mental and emotional disorder that needs to be properly addressed. It is charity that compels us to speak the truth and to seek authentic means that might help people with this dysphoria to order their feelings and experiences to reality.

Do we understand the gravity of the transgender movement and its various claims? Do we speak the truth in love and seek authentic help for anyone who is suffering?

"The human body shares in the dignity of 'the image of God': it is a human body precisely because it is animated by a spiritual soul, and it is the whole human person that is intended to become, in the body of Christ, a temple of the Spirit."

—*Catechism of the Catholic Church*, no. 364

Inconsistency of Argument

Truth is always consistent and wonderfully harmonious. The ancient Greeks defined beauty as the perfection of symmetry, acknowledging the peace that comes with a tranquility of order. With that in mind, any moral worldview that lacks consistency or interior coherence reveals its insufficiencies and errors.

If we apply this criterion to the LGBTQ+ movement, we see a glaring irregularity. Within the same movement, we are told that if someone is "gay," they cannot change who they are. If, however, someone has gender dysphoria, then they must change who they are and seek to become the person they think they should be. These two views are in conflict and indicate the cracks and errors in the moral worldview of the LGBTQ+ movement.

Do we appreciate the harmony of truth? Do we recognize the interior inconsistency within the LGBTQ+ movement?

Normalization of Disorder

In reviewing our approach to the LGBTQ+ movement, we need to address the very difficult subjects of consent, compromise, and accommodation. As Christians, we must not capitulate to our fallen culture. We must always speak the truth in love. By speaking truth, it is our great hope that people in the LGBTQ+ movement might recognize the true disorder that is causing them harm and then pursue a way of life that will free them from further hurt or injury.

Our fallen culture has succumbed to the pressure and vanity of the LGBTQ+ movement. As such, the vast majority of our social institutions have declared themselves "advocates" and have sought to normalize homosexuality and transgenderism.

The landscape in these areas is extensive. On one extreme, we have the legalization of gay "marriage," while on the other side, we have the cultural pressure of personal pronouns and access to restrooms. And there is much between that affects daily life, workplaces, neighborhoods, and public spaces.

As Christians, who know that God created us male and female and that the two genders have a beautiful complementarity, we are tasked to oppose these efforts at normalization. In doing so, we run the risk of receiving the full ire of "tolerant" people, who will call us terrible names and seek even social or legal action against us simply because we disagree with them. And yet, we are summoned to hold the line, to speak the truth in love, and to accept such offenses and persecutions as acts of love to God and our neighbor.

Since the LGBTQ+ movement now affects every aspect of our public lives, here are some specific questions and answers:

- Should family members who are living a homosexual lifestyle, or who are transgender, be invited to holiday celebrations?

    Yes, such members of the family should be invited, but not their gay partners, or only if they are addressed (and dress) according to their proper gender. If Uncle Carl wants to be called Aunt Carole, then they have passed on the invitation.

If Cousin Larry wants to bring his "husband,"
then he has passed on the invitation.

- Can I attend the gay "wedding" of a family member?
  Christians do not participate in gay "weddings"
  since they are an affront to natural married life.
  Christians cannot involve themselves in anything
  that might publicly normalize such a way of life.
  If the family member is open to it, there can be a
  respective and charitable conversation about why
  we cannot attend, while also expressing our love
  for them.

- Can I participate in a workplace party or congrat-
  ulations to a colleague who has entered into a gay
  "marriage"?
  We cannot participate in such things. While our
  absence might cause some misunderstanding and
  possible retribution, we cannot be involved in
  anything that would seek to normalize an active
  homosexual relationship.

- Should I use the new pronouns of a neighbor who
  has "transitioned" to a new gender?
  We cannot play along with such linguistic games.
  If necessary, we can use purposeful pluralized
  pronouns, but we should avoid anything that will
  publicly normalize such actions.

- Can my child participate in a slumber party hosted
  by a lesbian couple in my neighborhood?
  Christian parents guard the moral formation of
  their children and do not allow for the normalization of sexual deviancy. As such, Christian

children should not participate in any event hosted by a gay couple since such a relationship manipulates nature, redefines marriage, and does not model the natural understanding of family. It would cause needless confusion in the minds of children.

- Do we support gay adoption?

  As Christians, we do not support gay adoption. A homosexual couple is not the moral equivalent of a natural marriage of husband and wife. We know and strongly assert that every child deserves both a mother and father and the complementarity of their relationship.

These are only a few examples of common questions that arise in our contemporary culture. They are meant to give specific direction but also to help in forming a general guideline by which other questions can be discerned and answered.

"Let the enemy rage at the gate; let him knock, pound, scream, howl; let him do his worst. We know for certain that he cannot enter our soul except by the door of our consent."

—Saint Francis de Sales

LOVE IN THE TRENCHES

The range of questions relating to the LGBTQ+ movement requires serious knowledge and attention by believers. Christians and people of goodwill are to understand both the demands of justice in speaking the truth and the demands of charity in showing respect and kindness to all.

Love is the call to seek the good in others, even to accepting suffering on their behalf. In love, therefore, people of faith and goodwill respect the dignity of their neighbor, as they also seek the moral health and enrichment of the common good.

KEY TAKEAWAYS

As a quick reference, here are the key takeaways on the LGBTQ+ movement and complementarity:

- All human beings are loved by God and possess an incommunicable dignity that must be respected by all. No sin or life of sin can justify violence or harm against anyone.
- The human race consists of the male and female gender. The two possess an observable complementarity of body and soul.
- Disorders exist within our fallen world.
- The exclusive or predominant sexual attraction toward one's own gender is a disorder. A person cannot be disordered.
- The Church has no opinion on the genesis of homosexual attraction.
- Even if someone is born with homosexual attraction, it is still a disorder and cannot be acted upon.
- Homosexual attraction is not sinful in itself. Homosexual acts are always gravely sinful.
- Homosexual acts are not parallel with other sins against chastity since they violate nature. It is one of the rare sins known as "sins that cry to heaven for vengeance."

- People with a homosexual orientation are called to a life of chastity.
- The feeling or experience of disassociation with one's birth gender or physical characteristics relating to it is a disorder.

Going to the Mountain

Having presented our arguments, and always seeking to speak the truth in love, we now retreat and go to the mountain for prayer, spiritual rejuvenation, and supplication.

PRAYER

Heavenly Father,
In Your manifold goodness,
You created man and woman in Your own image,
And You blessed them with a beautiful complementarity.
Fill our hearts with wisdom and understanding.
Show us Your way of love.
Bless those who struggle with homosexual attractions
Or gender dysphoria.
Help them to know of Your love.
Guide them along Your way of truth.
We thank You and praise You!
Through Christ Our Lord.
Amen.

EXAMINATION OF CONSCIENCE

The following questions are given as help to examine our consciences on the issue of the LGBTQ+ and complementarity.

- Do I believe in the dignity of every human person, regardless of their moral status?
- Do I support natural marriage and programs that promote it in society?
- Do I believe in the nuclear family and argue for its status and rights in society?
- Do I pray for those who struggle with same-sex attraction or gender dysphoria?
- Do I defend natural marriage, or do I remain silent for human respectability?
- Have I become culturally complacent with the LGBTQ+ movement?
- Have I attended rallies or other events that support the LGBTQ+?
- Do I assert the sinfulness of homosexual acts and refuse to be a part of the normalization of the homosexual way of life?
- Do I speak the truth about gender dysphoria?
- Do I understand the depth and beauty of chastity?

Based on the insights of this examination of conscience, you're encouraged to go and make a good confession.

After reviewing this social issue, recommit yourself to the Lordship of Jesus Christ and ask for the intercession of your guardian angel.

"SUSCIPE" PRAYER

Take, Lord, and receive all my liberty,
my memory, my understanding,
and my entire will,
All I have and call my own.

You have given all to me.
To You, Lord, I return it.

Everything is Yours; do with it what You will.
Give me only Your love and Your grace,
that is enough for me.
Amen.

GUARDIAN ANGEL PRAYER

Angel of God,
My guardian dear,
To whom God's love
Commits me here.
Ever this day,
Be at my side,
To light and guard
To rule and guide.
Amen.

ADDED DEVOTIONAL

A suggested devotional: Pray the Joyful Mysteries of the Rosary, especially the third mystery: the birth of the Lord Jesus in Bethlehem. In your prayer, focus on the dignity of every human life, the restoration of that dignity in Jesus Christ, and the call we all have to recognize, defend, and cherish that dignity in others.

A suggested devotional: Pray the Stations of the Cross, especially the sixth station: Veronica wipes the face of Jesus. In your prayer, pray for the graces of conversion and peace among all those in the LGBTQ+ movement.

Suggested saintly intercessors: Saint Aelred of Rievaulx, Saint Peter Damian, Saint Mary of Egypt, Saint Charles Lwanga and Companions, and Saint Gemma Galgani.

"We are not the sum of our weaknesses and failures, we are the sum of the Father's love for us and our real capacity to become the image of His Son Jesus."

—Pope Saint John Paul II

"Love everyone with a deep love based on charity . . . but form friendships only with those who can share virtuous things with you. The higher the virtues you share and exchange with others, the more perfect your friendship will be."

—Saint Francis de Sales

CITATIONS FROM THE
CATECHISM OF THE CATHOLIC CHURCH

Charity: 1822–29
Complementarity: 2331–36
Creation: 279–324
Marriage: 2360–63
Human Dignity: 1700–15, 1929–30
Homosexuality: 2357–59, 2347

Chapter 5

Universal Healthcare and Subsidiarity

"[He] went to him and bound up his wounds, pouring on oil and wine; then he set him on his own beast and brought him to an inn, and took care of him. And the next day he took out two denarii and gave them to the innkeeper, saying, 'Take care of him; and whatever more you spend, I will repay you when I come back.'"
—Luke 10:34–35

Building a Foundation

Before we present the issue of universal healthcare, it's critical that we have a sense of virtue and some guiding principles from the Church's social doctrine.

Virtue: *Faith*
(see *CCC* 1814–16)

Faith is one of the core Christian virtues. It gives us the grace to believe in God, His revelation, and His words and deeds. By faith, the human person is able to commit his entire self to God. As such, faith requires works, such as service to the poor and sick. Without works, faith is dead.

PRINCIPLE: *NATURAL RIGHTS*
(SEE *CCC* 1928–48)

Natural rights are given by God and imbedded into human nature. They precede society and government. They are not given by any human authority. A person does not even give natural rights to himself and, therefore, cannot take them from himself. Natural rights are universal and held by every human person. Such rights must be respected by society's laws, public policies, and popular customs. Laws that violate or deny natural rights are unjust laws. Governments that offend or reject natural rights undermine their own moral legitimacy to govern.

A SECOND PRINCIPLE: *SUBSIDIARITY*
(SEE *CCC* 1883–85)

Subsidiarity is the principle by which human beings are called to express friendship and charity in a series of expanding relationships. Subsidiarity seeks out the most appropriate level for any given care or support. It seeks to be as close as possible to human relationships and avoids excessive interventions by higher relationships that can threaten personal freedom and initiative. As such, subsidiarity seeks to prevent a community of a higher order interfering in the internal life of a community of a lower order. Subsidiarity never deprives any community of its proper functions. It calls for support and coordination between higher and lower communities only when needed. It is a foundational principle of society and the common good.

Taking Our Stand

Since we have the assistance of virtue, and some principles from the Church's social doctrine, we are now ready to dive into the question of universal healthcare and subsidiarity.

THE KEY OF SUBSIDIARITY

During a conference some time ago, I went for a coffee with a friend during a break from the talks. While we were both enjoying our drinks, the topic of universal healthcare came up. I was caught off guard that my friend, whom I hadn't seen in a while, was against the notion of healthcare for all. I expressed my surprise and asked, "Don't you believe there is a human right for healthcare?"

He was honest and replied, "I don't know."

I followed up my question with another. "Don't you believe that any person who is hurting has a right to receive some form of care to keep him from suffering?"

He smiled. "Yes, of course. When you put it that way, it's pretty obvious. I'm just not sure about it becoming a political issue."

"Okay," I responded. "I agree."

"You do?"

"Yes, as Catholics, we believe in a basic human right to healthcare. We believe that some type of healthcare should be provided for any person who is suffering, but we also believe in subsidiarity."

My friend was familiar with the principle of subsidiarity. Once I mentioned it, he perked up. "Yes, yes, exactly! That's my point. Of course, I don't want anyone to suffer, but I also don't want the federal government handling it and telling us what to do."

And he was spot on. Catholic social doctrine certainly argues for universal healthcare. It's been our issue for some time. But our social doctrine also believes in subsidiarity—namely, that the lowest appropriate level of authority and community should address the issue and propose prudential ways in which healthcare can be provided. It's not the place of the federal government to facilitate such care. It's dangerous to entrust healthcare to a removed national government. It lends itself to socialized medicine, which is opposed to Catholic social doctrine.

In general, after proposing the key of subsidiarity, the issue of universal healthcare oftentimes becomes more digestible and realistic to people. Of course, subsidiarity only suggests a way. The specifics and logistics to universal healthcare will still need to be addressed and resolved. Such resolutions, however, must ensure that the dignity of every human life is respected, the right to healthcare is prudentially provided, and no human being—made in God's image—is left to needlessly suffer.

In our discipleship, do we attempt to alleviate the sufferings of others? Do we understand how universal healthcare is connected to human dignity? Are we also committed to subsidiarity in providing healthcare to others?

> "As long as any one has the means of doing good
> to his neighbors, and does not do so, he shall be
> reckoned a stranger to the love of the Lord."
>
> —Saint Irenaeus of Lyons

The Care of the Human Body

As the Psalmist announces: "I praise you, for I am wondrously made. Wonderful are your works! You know me right well (Ps 139:14). This great creation includes our bodies. They share in the dignity of our nature and cooperate with our spiritual soul in our desire for an abundant, holy life.

Since the body is created by God, it merits our attention and protection. We are morally obliged to care for our bodies. This includes seeking medical attention when necessary. It also means following medical counsel and taking proper medication when prescribed. The care of our bodies also includes avoiding any kinds of excess, such as with food, alcohol, tobacco, prescription medication, popular drugs, sexual activity, elective surgical procedures, adrenaline highs, and other such things.

"Life and physical health are precious gifts entrusted to us by God. We must take reasonable care of them, taking into account the needs of others and the common good."

—*Catechism of the Catholic Church*, no. 2288

"Regarding your bodily health, obey the orders of the physician. Tell him sincerely what you suffer, in modest, clear, and concise language; after having said all that is necessary, be silent and let him act. Do not refuse remedies, but take them in the loving chalice of Jesus, with a pleasant countenance. Be grateful to the person who nurses you; take whatever she offers you. In brief, act as a child in the arms of its mother. Remain in your bed as on the cross. Jesus prayed for three hours on the cross, and His was a truly crucified prayer, with no comfort from within or without."

—Saint Paul of the Cross

By extension, solidarity calls us to share in the responsibility of assisting our neighbors in being attentive and caring for their bodies. Concurrently, subsidiarity calls us to be prudent in the exercise of this moral obligation.

Do we realize the dignity of our bodies? Does the care we give to our bodies reflect this dignity? Do we understand the balance between solidarity and subsidiarity in the prudential discernment of how to assist our neighbors in the care of their bodies?

> "All our religion is but a false religion, and all our virtues are mere illusions and we ourselves are only hypocrites in the sight of God, if we have not that universal charity for everyone—for the good, and for the bad, for the poor and for the rich, and for all those who do us harm as much as those who do us good."
>
> —Saint John Vianney

A Basic Human Right

As God has created each person in His own image and likeness, we each share an incommunicable dignity. This dignity, grounded in our very nature as human persons, brings forth certain rights (and responsibilities). These rights cannot be taken away by any government or set of laws. Good government and just laws are good and just precisely because they defer, protect, and nurture the expression of these rights.

The common good of a society is built upon the mutual recognition of these rights and the shared responsibility of all persons to exercise them in their own lives and to support their neighbor in their own exercise of these rights. Among the rights of each human being is the right to medical attention and healthcare. If a person is suffering and care is available, the person has a natural right to receive that care.

Of course, such statements are broad, and there are many specific questions that need prudential discernment and decision. For example, what level of care is required under this natural right? Is urgent care sufficient? Can the level of care be determined by the age and/or health of a person? To what degree is extensive, long-term care included in this right? Who is responsible for the expenses of this medical care? If the expenses of such care are covered by citizens, what level of medical care is morally required for non-citizens? And the list continues. Each of these questions requires serious consideration, debate, and decision by those in authority.

Do I recognize the natural rights within human nature? Do I demand that such rights be respected in my society and by my political leadership? Do I understand the intricacies and the prudence involved in making decisions on healthcare questions?

"Concern for the health of its citizens requires that
society help in the attainment of living-conditions
that allow them to grow and reach maturity:
food and clothing, housing, health care, basic
education, employment, and social assistance."

—*Catechism of the Catholic Church*, no. 2288

Cautious Toward Government

Among the questions relating to universal healthcare is the poignant inquiry on who or what entity should facilitate the coverage of medical treatment and care. The language of universal healthcare has regrettably been hijacked and falsely associated with a federalized, socialized healthcare program.

In her social doctrine, the Church does not favor the government running health or human services. Flowing from the principle of subsidiarity, the Church prefers intermediary groups. Such groups are intermediary because they are between the government and the individual citizen. Examples of intermediary groups include labor unions or other work associations, professional organizations, religious-based alliances, neighborhood consortiums, locally-based cooperatives, cultural leagues, and civic or service institutions.

In the realm of healthcare, the Church's principal focus is to ensure the best possible attention to each person in need of medical treatment and care. In addition, the Church's focus is a historically learned suspicion and cautionary approach to government—especially large government—running health and human services. Such control by a government over a required and pressing need of the people under its jurisdiction is a precarious arrangement since it affords government too much authority. If government must be involved, however, the Church favors local government so that it is immediately obliged and directly accountable to those under its authority.

The question remains, therefore, over who or what entity should provide coverage for healthcare. Any efforts by our national government to bypass subsidiarity and to socialize healthcare must be challenged and prevented. In no moral universe is universal healthcare the proper provenance of a federal government.

Ask yourself: Am I involved in intermediary groups? Do I realize their importance in the Church's social doctrine? Do I understand the Church's cautionary stance about government running health and human services?

"It is incumbent on those who exercise authority
to strengthen the values that inspire the confidence
of the members of the group and encourage
them to put themselves at the service of others.
Participation begins with education and culture."

—*Catechism of the Catholic Church*, no. 1917

"The dignity of the human person requires the
pursuit of the common good. Everyone should
be concerned to create and support institutions
that improve the conditions of human life."

—*Catechism of the Catholic Church*, no. 1926

"The Church has rejected the totalitarian
and atheistic ideologies associated in modern
times with 'communism' or 'socialism.'"

—*Catechism of the Catholic Church*, no. 2425

FAITH IN THE TRENCHES

The question of universal healthcare requires serious discernment of the principles within the Church's social doctrine and mature prudential judgments by those in authority. Christians and people of goodwill understand the moral responsibility of caring for those who are sick and suffering.

Faith calls us to believe in God, who can neither deceive nor be deceived. Faith, therefore, demands a surrender of our lives to God and the performance of good works. Such good works include service to the sick, ill, and suffering. Faith relies on the other virtues, including prudence, to know how best to perform and implement such good works.

Key Takeaways

As a quick reference, here are the key takeaways on universal healthcare and subsidiarity:

- Every human person is made in the image and likeness of God.
- Our bodies are an integral part of our personhood. They share in the dignity of our nature.
- Our human nature was endowed by God with certain natural rights.
- Our natural rights preceded society and government. No human authority can take away or legitimately repress these rights.
- Solidarity and subsidiarity are necessary in understanding and exercising these natural rights.
- Each person bears the moral responsibility to care for his body and to help his neighbor in his duty to care for his body.
- Our natural rights include healthcare.
- Prudence is needed in answering the multiple questions relating to the exercise of this right.
- The Church favors intermediary groups in covering healthcare and medical needs.
- The Church is cautious about government-run health and human services. She is opposed to socialized medicine.

Going to the Mountain

Having presented our arguments, and always seeking to speak the truth in love, we now retreat and go to the mountain for prayer, spiritual rejuvenation, and supplication.

PRAYER

Good and Gracious God,
You are the Healer and Physician
Of our souls and of our bodies.
Come to us in our need.
You call us to care for our bodies.
You ask us to assist our neighbor
As they care for their bodies.
Bless our efforts.
Enlighten our minds.
Console those who suffer.
Grant peace to those in distress.
Heal those who are hurting.
Guide us with Your love.
We adore You. We trust You.
For You are Lord, forever and ever.
Amen.

EXAMINATION OF CONSCIENCE

The following questions are given as help to examine our consciences on the issue of universal healthcare and subsidiarity.

- Do I acknowledge the dignity of every human being?
- Do I pray for a better world in which those who suffer can receive help?

- Do I take care of my body?
- Have I indulged in some form of excess in the care of my body?
- Do I support my neighbor in his efforts to care for his body?
- Do I regularly see medical professionals in an effort to care for my body?
- Do I support the right of all people to see medical personnel when they're suffering?
- Do I understand the intricacies of the prudential judgments involved in the realm of universal healthcare?
- Have I been active in intermediary groups in my society?
- Do I have a healthy suspicion of government facilitating health and human services?

Based on the insights of this examination of conscience, you're encouraged to go and make a good confession.

After reviewing this social issue, recommit yourself to the Lordship of Jesus Christ and ask for the intercession of your guardian angel.

"SUSCIPE" PRAYER

Take, Lord, and receive all my liberty,
my memory, my understanding,
and my entire will,
All I have and call my own.

You have given all to me.
To You, Lord, I return it.

Everything is Yours; do with it what You will.
Give me only Your love and Your grace,
that is enough for me.
Amen.

GUARDIAN ANGEL PRAYER

Angel of God,
My guardian dear,
To whom God's love
Commits me here.
Ever this day,
Be at my side,
To light and guard
To rule and guide.
Amen.

ADDED DEVOTIONAL

A suggested devotional: Pray the Luminous Mysteries of the Rosary, especially the third mystery: the proclamation of the Kingdom of God. In your prayer, focus on the dignity of every human life, the immense care of the Lord Jesus of the sick and suffering during His public ministry, and the summons we all have to prudently work for healthcare coverage for all.

A suggested devotional: Pray the Stations of the Cross, especially the second station: Jesus accepts His cross. In your prayer, pray for the sick and suffering, especially for those who are in need of proper medical coverage.

Suggested saintly intercessors: Saint Luke, Saints Cosmas and Damian, Saint Camillus de Lellis, Saint Vincent de Paul, and Saint Joseph Moscati.

"Love the poor tenderly, regarding them as your masters and yourselves as their servants."

—Saint John of God

"Show me your hands. Do they have scars from giving? Show me your feet. Are they wounded in service? Show me your heart. Have you left a place for divine love?"

—Venerable Fulton J. Sheen

CITATIONS FROM THE
CATECHISM OF THE CATHOLIC CHURCH

Faith: 1814–16
Natural Rights: 1928–48
Solidarity: 1939–42
Intermediate Groups: 1882–83, 1893–94, 1910
Christ the Physician: 1503–05
Human Dignity: 1700–15, 1929–30
Natural Rights: 1928–48
Respect for Life: 2258–62
Respect for Health: 2288–91
Person and Society: 1877–96
Common Good: 1905–17
Excess: 2290

Chapter 6

Artificial Nutrition/ Hydration and Mercy

"Then the righteous will answer him, 'Lord, when was it that we saw you hungry and feed you, or thirsty and give you drink?'"
—*Matthew 25:37*

Building a Foundation

Before we present the issue of nutrition and hydration, it's critical that we have a sense of virtue and some guiding principles from the Church's social doctrine.

Virtue: *Temperance*
(see *CCC* 1809)

Temperance is a high moral virtue. It helps us to moderate our attraction to pleasures. It guides us to find a balance in the use of created goods in our life. Temperance helps us to have a mastery over our instincts. It empowers us to keep our desires within what is good and honorable. It prevents manipulation or exaggeration, as it orders our emotions and points us to what is truly noble and virtuous.

PRINCIPLE: *MERCY*
(SEE *CCC* 210–11, 270–71, 1037, 1473,
1847, 1994, 2100, 2447, 2840)

As a social principle, mercy is an accentuated expression of solidarity. It focuses on our call to fellowship and harmony with one another. It includes the forgiveness of sins and the restoration of communion, but it is also much broader. It involves patience, kindness, and faithfulness, as well as an acceptance of sufferings and trials of all kinds and the coming to the aid of another in their necessities.

A SECOND PRINCIPLE: *HUMAN DIGNITY*
(SEE *CCC* 27, 306–8, 356–57, 364, 369, 872, 1004,
1700–15, 1730, 1929–30, 1934, 2158, 2203, 2334)

The principle of human dignity asserts that every human person is made in the image of God, that every human being is a someone, not a something. As such, every human person has the power to act on their own and is capable of self-knowledge, of self-possession, and of freely giving himself and entering into communion with other persons. Human dignity upholds that the human person is an intelligent and free cause who, by knowledge and love, can share in God's own life. While such dignity can regrettably be eclipsed and offended, it cannot be taken away by any created entity, including the person himself.

Taking Our Stand

Since we have the assistance of virtue, and some principles from the Church's social doctrine, we are now ready to dive into the question of artificial nutrition/hydration and mercy.

"I Don't Want to Be a Burden . . ."

Oftentimes in dealing with those who are terminally ill, or with those who are facing long-term medical treatment, I've heard them say, "I don't want to be a burden to my children!" Trying to break the tension, I'll often reply, "You're too late! You've been a burden to them since the day they were born!"

The comment usually provokes a laugh or a confused look. But the point is made. Love is filled with burdens. Relationships are overflowing with burdens. Saint Paul tells us, "Bear one another's burdens, and so fulfill the law of Christ" (Gal 6:2).

It's true that the term *burden* can be applied to love and relationships, but it's also true—and we have to be careful of this distinction—that it should never be applied to a person. People are not burdens. Each of us is made in the image and likeness of God (see Gn 1:26–28). Simply put, God is our Father and we look like Him. This identity bestows on all of us an inalienable dignity that must be respected and cherished, even in the midst of the burdens and exhaustion that are a part of giving care (or receiving it).

This basic point has to be made since we live in a culture intoxicated with utilitarianism, which is the belief that value is only found in what we can receive or in what we can get from someone else. We live in a culture that has taught people that any inconvenience for another person, or any service that makes us uncomfortable, is unmerited. We're told that the recipient of such care is a burden, especially those who are the most vulnerable and weak among us. Many in our culture have bought this lie.

In contrast to our society's utilitarianism, Christian teaching has always asserted that the only adequate response to a person is love (see Jn 13:34–35). By focusing on love—seeking the good in others—we can expose selfishness that disguises itself as mercy. We can break a downward spiral that overemphasizes the hardship of loved ones to the neglect of the person who is principally suffering. And so, it is true love for another, made in God's image, that helps us see the person's dignity. This realization calls us to order our own emotions and difficulties according to the other person's dignity. It liberates us from self-absorption and helps us see the good that is being done and the beauty that is being defended.

Do we unmask the lie of our fallen culture that tells people that they are a burden? Do we understand the difference between the real burdens of love and the false claim that people are burdens?

"I will never tire of repeating this: what the poor need the most is not pity but love. They need to feel respect for their human dignity, which is neither less nor different from the dignity of any other human being."

—Saint Teresa of Calcutta

THE IMAGE OF GOD

For the Christian believer, creation is the foundation of God's saving work, which is fulfilled in Jesus Christ. The world was created for our good, and we were created because of God's love for us. This point is worth stressing: We are not a *something* but a *someone*, and we only exist because God loves us. If God ceased to love us, we would completely disappear. All that we are, including our history, family, and health, dwells in existence because of God's love.

The living God seals His love for us by placing His very own image and likeness within us. Unlike the angels or the animals, we bear a special mark that identifies us as the sons and daughters of God. We are consecrated and dedicated to Him and His glory. Our lives are temples of His majesty and witnesses to His care for creation. The image that we each bear is a singular narrative all its own. No one else can repeat or duplicate who we are. No one else can reveal what we can disclose about God since the image we have of Him is unrepeatable (see Ps 8:4–8).

Understood in this light, the Christian is comfortable acknowledging that every human life is a true gift from God. Life is the first and highest of all gifts since it is the means by which all other gifts are received. But life is also a fragile gift entrusted to the person who receives it, to his family and community, and to the entire human race. Life, therefore, is a gift that is also a sacred responsibility.

In my life, do I acknowledge the dignity of every human being? Do I question the dignity of others when I see life in its most vulnerable or distressing phases? Do I accuse myself of such thoughts and affirm that every human person is made in God's image?

"Each one of them is Jesus in disguise."

—Saint Teresa of Calcutta

BODY AND SOUL

As human beings made in God's image, we consist of a body and a soul. Both our bodies and our souls share in the image of God. The body is not to be diminished, dismissed as some raw matter with no identity, or merely seen as a vehicle that carries our souls around. No, the body shares in our dignity. It must therefore be respected, cared for, and properly esteemed. Our souls should not be approached as somehow our "true selves," as if the body was a foreign component to our personhood. Such a false view has rationalized all sorts of medical neglect, disordered compassion, calculated harm, and willful manipulation of our bodies.

The complementarity of our souls and bodies are reflected in many ways, especially when we love, express delight, give thanks, and suffer. For example, our souls share in the sufferings of our bodies and vice versa. If our body has a high temperature, then our will is weakened and virtue is more difficult. If our souls are clouded with melancholy, then our bodies experience a weakening of muscle capacity.

In discerning medical treatment and care, therefore, we have to be cautious not to isolate the soul from the body, or the body from the soul. As human beings, we are both body and soul, and the care we give ourselves, or receive from others, must consider both these portions of our personhood.

Do I reflect and seek to have wonder over the beauty of our creation as human beings? Do I fully acknowledge the body's dignity with the soul, and vice versa?

"The human body shares in the dignity of 'the image of God': it is a human body precisely because it is animated by a spiritual soul, and it is the whole human person that is intended to become, in the body of Christ, a temple of the Spirit."

—*Catechism of the Catholic Church*, no. 364

DYING WITH DIGNITY

In making end-of-life decisions, some people will say, "I just want to die with dignity." And they will. We all do. Our dignity is not given by our health, autonomy, by laws or government, or even by ourselves. Our dignity is given to us by our Creator. It is inalienable. No one, no thing, can take it away. Therefore, this inalienable dignity demands respect. It is the foundation of our human vocation, our call to live as full human beings, cherishing, respecting, and flourishing within our own dignity and that of others.

This means that, in terms of end-of-life planning, while we must discern many things in the realm of treatment, we have boundaries. Our personal will, or the desire for autonomy, are not sovereign. These must be placed within our human dignity and the objective order of moral goodness, which is binding on all people of goodwill (and is seen as a manifestation of God's will by believers). This shows us that we cannot take our own lives or cause willful harm to our well-being.

Do I hold firm to the fundamental dignity of every human life? Do I speak and argue for this truth in society?

"Life, especially human life, belongs to God; whoever attacks human life attacks God's very self."

—Pope Saint John Paul II, encyclical
Evangelium Vitae, no. 9

QUALITY OF LIFE VERSUS HUMAN DIGNITY

Given our identity as human persons and our existential connection to God, we have to understand that our self-possession, popularly called autonomy, is not an absolute power. Our autonomy is dependent; it has to make reference to God and His providential design of our bodies and souls, as well as His divine law and the family and community to which He has entrusted us. Our autonomy, therefore, should never be viewed as independent from our dignity as children of God.

Our definition of "quality of life" is not simply the power to live however we want in whatever way we want. Seen holistically and in light of our transcendence as the children of God, our quality of life is grounded upon our dignity. It is matured by love and an openness to live with inconvenience, discomfort, imperfection, and suffering. Our quality of life is improved through a willingness to surrender what we prefer for the sake of what is good and in accord with our dignity as the children of God.

Have I recognized a wayward autonomy in my own heart? Do I sometimes allow a supposed quality of life to over-shadow a person's dignity? Do I recognize such thoughts and reorient my thinking so that I understand (and defend) the dignity of every human person?

"The intrinsic value and personal dignity of every human being does not change depending on their circumstances."

—Pope Saint John Paul II, Address at Lourdes, France, August 16, 2004

ORDINARY AND EXTRAORDINARY CARE

As Christian disciples, we desire to do what the Lord asks of us and to do it with trust and joy. Our discernment helps us discover and determine what the best course of care might be in light of the Lord's will for us in each situation. Our discernment, therefore, always addresses a specific state of affairs, in a particular place, and at a specific time.

There are two expressions that help to clarify what we are called to do:

- *Ordinary* care is that care which is morally *obligatory*.
- *Extraordinary* care is that care which is morally *optional*.

The distinction between the two is essential for our discernment since ordinary care is the summons of the Lord. We are called to abandon all things and to give an obedience of faith to these areas of our end-of-life care. It would be severely regrettable if a person were to have lived their entire life as a faithful Christian but then abandon the cross and the demands of discipleship at the end of life. In order to prevent this scandal, each of us is obliged to enter into serious discernment, seek counsel, and to do whatever the Lord asks of us.

It's worth remembering that we do not determine, but merely discern, what is morally good. Our discernment is marked by our faith in the Lord Jesus and His Church, which is guided by the Holy Spirit.

It's natural to ask, in acknowledging our human vocation and our particular vocation, how we can discern what is ordinary or extraordinary. Is it possible that something is obligatory to one person but not to another? Are these terms applied to specific medical procedures or types of treatment?

The distinction between ordinary and extraordinary care can be seen as a comparison of benefits and burdens. This means our discernment must involve some "practicals," such as the possibility of survival or benefit to one's person, the degree of possible side effects, the extent of the proposed treatment, our capacity for pain, our responsibilities to other people or society, and our financial means. Within the boundaries set by moral truth, we have to add these other factors into the arena as we decide whether we are obliged to accept treatment or not.

Since our discernment follows our particular vocation, it is possible that a medical procedure or treatment is obligatory for one while optional for another. Within the boundaries set by our human vocation, we cannot solely identify a specific medical procedure or treatment as ordinary or extraordinary. While the medical community may do so and use the same terms, the Church uses these terms far more holistically and calls for us to consider many areas of our life and not simply the medical intervention that is being proposed.

And so, we seek to know what the Lord is asking of us and then generously respond with trust and confidence. The Lord will never overwhelm us or abandon us. He will only give us what we can carry. But, in order to carry what He gives us, we must rely on Him and the workings of His grace.

Do I understand the difference between ordinary and extraordinary care? Do I realize the intricacies that are involved in discerning whether something is ordinary and extraordinary?

"Discontinuing medical procedures that are burdensome, dangerous, extraordinary, or disproportionate to the expected outcome can be legitimate; it is the refusal of 'over-zealous' treatment. Here one does not will to cause death; one's inability to impede it is merely accepted. The decisions should be made by the patient if he is competent and able or, if not, by those legally entitled to act for the patient, whose reasonable will and legitimate interests must always be respected."

—*Catechism of the Catholic Church*, no. 2278

ARTIFICIAL NUTRITION AND HYDRATION

Food and water are basic human needs, even if provided artificially. Unfortunately, many in the medical community will designate artificial nutrition and hydration as extraordinary care in and of themselves. Contrary to this view, artificially administered food and water are not in themselves extraordinary care. They are within the realm of basic human care.

Giving food or water to another person is always a charitable act and one that parallels a basic human need. Only in situations when the body is unable to assimilate them (or they become harmful to the patient) are artificially administered food and water classified as extraordinary care and properly suspended.

We can imagine our reaction if someone were to refuse to change a terminally ill person's adult diaper or bedding because "they're going to die anyway." We would rightly be appalled. We expect that these basic human services would be provided until the person actually dies. In a similar way, this is how moral truth approaches food and water. It's a service that is not negotiable so long as the person's body can receive and benefit from the food and water, even if these are given artificially.

The fact that a person is unable to feed himself or drink water himself and must, therefore, be provided these basic human needs artificially does not—in any way—preclude medical professionals or family members from providing this basic care to the patient.

Do I realize that I am obliged to give food and drink to any other human being, even if such care is artificially given? Do I understand that those who suffer and need assistance are a great blessing to myself and society?

"If you can't feed a hundred people, then feed just one."

—Saint Teresa of Calcutta

Suspended Care?

Every human person has dignity and a human vocation, which is a call to live and cherish our shared humanity. This acknowledgment of human dignity, and of our solidarity as human beings with one another, demands that we generously provide basic human care, which includes food and water (even if administered artificially). If we stop these basic needs, then we are starving or dehydrating the person to death. This would be euthanasia since it is the deprivation of food and water that are causing death rather than the person's illness or medical condition.

The only time that food and hydration can be suspended is when a person's body is unable to assimilate them and/or they cause harm to the person. In these cases, the good offered by food and water would not actually be serving any good and so they must be suspended. This would not be euthanasia since the person's medical condition is causing death and not the suspension of food and water.

This last point must be emphasized. In the discernment of when to suspend nutrition and hydration (even if artificially administered), the rule of thumb is the pressing question: *What will cause the death of this person?* If death occurs because of the removal of food and water, then it is euthanasia. If, however, death is caused by the person's medical condition or illness, then it is not euthanasia (even if food and water had to be suspended toward the end of life because of the illness and the inability of the body to assimilate them).

Do I understand when and under what circumstances care can be suspended? Do I realize the importance of being attentive to each part of such a discernment process? Do I appreciate the dying process and acknowledge the afterlife?

> "Even if death is thought imminent, the ordinary care owed to a sick person cannot be legitimately interrupted. The use of painkillers to alleviate the sufferings of the dying, even at the risk of shortening their days, can be morally in conformity with human dignity if death is not willed as either an end or a means, but only foreseen and tolerated as inevitable palliative care is a special form of disinterested charity. As such it should be encouraged."
>
> —*Catechism of the Catholic Church*, no. 2279

RESPONSE TO MEDICAL PRESSURE

The majority of people in the medical profession are there because they sincerely wish to help people, and so we should always seek to approach them with respect and appropriate deference. At times, however, certain medical professionals overstep appropriate bounds and apply improper pressure to patients, medical proxies, and families.

The intentions behind such unseemly behavior are diverse. For some medical personnel, they are raw utilitarians and disregard spiritual or religious considerations. They can become impatient and dismissive to patients or proxies who try to explain their discernment of the person's dignity beyond just their abilities or functions. For other medical personnel, they might be open to spiritual considerations but have no developed understanding of Catholic teaching and the reasons behind it. This could even include some

Catholic medical professionals who do not know their faith as well as they know their medical practice.

Regardless of the reasons, the Christian patient or proxy must be steadfast. In the face of possible condescension and pressure, we are called to be advocates who can provide answers with explanations, apply our answers to the medical options presented, and ask the medical personnel to respect both our beliefs and our decisions.

If medical personnel continue to put pressure on a patient or proxy, they should request to see a patient advocate and/ or ask to have a different doctor. No one, especially someone who is sick or emotionally distressed, should be taken advantage of and have their beliefs and decisions derided or dismissed. Medical professionals are in service to the sick, and they should always revere the decisions of their patients (and proxies), especially when their decisions are based on holistic reasons such as their spiritual or religious worldview. Additionally, any patient or proxy can request to see a Catholic priest who can clarify our teachings and give support to the Catholic party.

Am I willing to stand up for what is right? Am I willing to defend the vulnerable and those who cannot defend themselves? Do I have the humility to ask for help and advocacy?

"Be brave, do not be led by what others think or say!"

—Saint John Bosco

REDEMPTIVE SUFFERING

No discussion of human life, or the practice of medicine, would be complete without addressing the full array of suffering not only within the soul but also in the body. In experiencing the fullness of human life, Jesus Christ understood and accepted all forms of suffering, and He desires to teach humanity (including the medical professional) the scope and truths surrounding human suffering.

As we saw, since humanity's fall from grace, suffering has been an evil within human life. Christian theology has always seen suffering as an evil and as a consequence of the original sin of Adam and Eve. In taking on our human nature, Jesus Christ accepted the suffering of humanity, *both* body and soul. From His life of poverty, to living as a refugee in a foreign land, to being hunted down as a criminal, to the frustration of learning a trade, to the death of His foster father, to His experience of fatigue and thirst, to being misunderstood, rejected, and unloved. All of His sufferings culminated in the cruelty and torture of His passion and the humiliation and asphyxiation of His death. In all these sufferings, He chose to accept, enter, and use suffering, which has been such a pivotal dilemma and source of anguish in human history, as the very means to manifest His love and self-donation for humanity. *Suffering itself would become the instrument of salvation.*

How is this possible? How did Jesus Christ use suffering for the redemption and renewal of humanity? In taking on human suffering, the Lord Jesus went directly to sin, understood as the source of suffering in human life. In order to take away sin and vanquish its control on humanity, Jesus Christ became sin itself. He sought to destroy this privation of being, and its consequences of suffering and death. In becoming sin, Jesus Christ took upon Himself all the sins of humanity throughout time. He endured the totality of human guilt, shame, alienation, grief, confusion, and the full panorama of darkness caused by sin.

The crucible for this radically human endeavor was the Lord's passion, which began in the Garden of Gethsemane. In the garden, as he took upon Himself the sins of humanity, the Lord Jesus sweated blood, felt the full isolation caused by sin, and could not raise His eyes to the heavens. In the Garden of Gethsemane, Jesus proved His association with suffering humanity and began His passion, which would ultimately destroy the power of sin and death through His death and resurrection.

On account of the unique depth of His human experience, Jesus Christ—true God and true Man—has complete credibility as the exemplar of what it means to be human. Additionally, His singular experiential knowledge of suffering in soul and body makes Him the standard by which both the care of the sick and suffering can be evaluated and its moral discernment measured.

But if Jesus Christ has destroyed sin, why does illness and suffering still afflict humanity? How is humanity (and the medical community) to understand suffering in light of the ministry of Jesus Christ?

We must understand that while the ministry of Jesus Christ has destroyed the kingdom of sin and death, the consequences of sin still remain in the human experience. The difference, however, is that suffering—while an evil caused by original sin—can now become redemptive for the person and the community. Rather than seeing suffering in merely negative terms, the example and ministry of Jesus Christ now shows the human family a positive way in which suffering can be seen and accepted.

Now, in Jesus Christ, suffering can be a source of repentance, purification, goodness, penance, renewal, hope, and empathy to others who are sick or suffering in some way. In the Lord Jesus, who offered His sufferings as a self-oblation and as a means of selfless service, humanity can see suffering as a new way of service to others and as a new means of self-donation and salvation for themselves and the whole world.

Do I approach suffering with a redemptive heart and mindset? Am I willing to suffer for a greater good? Do I offer up my suffering for my salvation and the redemption of others?

"For Jesus Christ I am prepared to suffer still more. And let us not forget that Jesus not only suffered, but also rose in glory; so, too, we go to the glory of the Resurrection by way of suffering and the Cross."

—Saint Maximilian Kolbe

TEMPERANCE IN THE TRENCHES

The question of artificial nutrition and hydration requires sound knowledge and attentive discernment of the principles of the Church's social doctrine. The prudential distinction between ordinary and extraordinary care is crucial to the morality of a course of action. Christians and people of goodwill must realize the intricacies of the matters involved in this level of care for those who are sick and suffering.

Temperance calls us to order our emotions and intellect according to truth. It calls us to a reliance on our will and prevents us from betraying goodness. It helps us to properly deal with and direct our fatigue, fear, and anxieties toward noble decisions that respect human dignity and proper human care. Temperance unmasks false mercy. It assists in assuaging our souls, as well as our perception and decision-making within a specific situation, so that truth and goodness triumph. Temperance relies on the other virtues, especially prudence.

Key Takeaways

As a quick reference, here are the key takeaways on artificial nutrition/hydration and mercy:

- While providing care to others might entail certain burdens, no person himself is a burden. The care is the burden, not the person.
- All human beings are made in the image of God and possess an inalienable dignity.
- Every human person dies with dignity. Nothing in this world can remove their dignity since it comes directly from our Creator.
- Our bodies and souls are united in our single personhood. They cannot be separated to justify harm or suspension of care to our bodies.
- Human dignity is not synonymous with quality of care. While we hope for a good quality of life, it does not justify euthanasia or any other offense to human dignity.

- Ordinary care is morally obligatory. Extraordinary care is morally optional. Prudence and discernment based on truth is essential in identifying whether a state of affairs is ordinary or extraordinary.
- All human persons share a human vocation and are summoned to provide basic human care to each other.
- Food and drink are included in basic human care, even if they are artificially administered.
- There are times in which extraordinary care allows for the suspension of care and for the natural dying process to play itself out.
- When we suffer, we can offer up our sufferings and sorrows with Jesus Christ and allow them to become redemptive for ourselves, for our loved ones, and for the whole Church.

Going to the Mountain

Having presented our arguments, and always seeking to speak the truth in love, we now retreat and go to the mountain for prayer, spiritual rejuvenation, and supplication.

Prayer

Eternal Father,
You are the Caregiver of all.
You love us and accompany us through life.
Come to us in our need!
Heal us from our fears and anxieties.
Strengthen us to care for others,
To give food and drink to others,

To sacrifice for others,
To selflessly serve others.
Grant us peace!
Help us to know Your will.
Show us Your love and mercy.
Through Christ Our Lord.
Amen.

EXAMINATION OF CONSCIENCE

The following questions are given as help to examine our consciences on the issue of artificial nutrition and hydration:

- Do I sometimes view other human beings as burdens?
- Do I take care of those under my responsibility?
- Do I acknowledge the dignity of every human being?
- Do I accept the difference between human dignity and quality of life?
- Do I develop virtue in my life so that I can holistically discern God's will?
- Do I live out my human vocation in caring for other people?
- Have I refused food or drink to others?
- Do I fulfill all of the demands of ordinary care?
- Do I accept the times when the natural dying process is called to play itself out?
- Do I offer up my sufferings for the benefit of others?

Based on the insights of this examination of conscience, you're encouraged to go and make a good confession.

After reviewing this social issue, recommit yourself to the Lordship of Jesus Christ and ask for the intercession of your guardian angel.

"Suscipe" Prayer

Take, Lord, and receive all my liberty,
my memory, my understanding,
and my entire will,
All I have and call my own.

You have given all to me.
To You, Lord, I return it.

Everything is Yours; do with it what You will.
Give me only Your love and Your grace,
that is enough for me.
Amen.

Guardian Angel Prayer

Angel of God,
My guardian dear,
To whom God's love
Commits me here.
Ever this day,
Be at my side,
To light and guard
To rule and guide.
Amen.

Added Devotional

A suggested devotional: Pray the Luminous Mysteries of the Rosary, especially the fifth mystery: the institution of the Eucharist. In your prayer, focus on the dignity of every human life, the immense care of the Lord Jesus for the sick and suffering, and the vocation we all have to care for one another and to provide basic human needs to our neighbors.

A suggested devotional: Pray the Stations of the Cross, especially the fifth station: Simon helps Jesus to carry His cross. In your prayer, remember the dying and their families, especially those who need help in understanding human dignity and assistance in the care of their loved ones.

Suggested saintly intercessors: Saint Nicholas of Myra, Saint Peter Claver, Saint Marianne Cope, Saint Frances of Rome, Saint Elizabeth of Hungary, Saint Vincent de Paul, and Saint Jane Frances de Chantal.

"Therefore every threat to human dignity and life must necessarily be felt in the Church's very heart; it cannot but affect her at the core of her faith in the Redemptive Incarnation of the Son of God, and engage her in her mission of proclaiming the Gospel of life in all the world and to every creature."

—Pope Saint John Paul II

"It is not Death that will come to fetch me, it is the good God. Death is no phantom, no horrible specter, as presented in pictures."

—Saint Therese the Little Flower

CITATIONS FROM THE
CATECHISM OF THE CATHOLIC CHURCH

Temperance: 1809

Mercy: 210–11, 270–71, 1037, 1473, 1847, 1994, 2100, 2447, 2840

Human Dignity: 27, 306, 308, 356–57, 364, 369, 872, 1004, 1700–15, 1730, 1929–30, 1934, 2158, 2203, 2334

Natural Rights: 1928–48

Solidarity: 1939–42

Christ the Physician: 1503–5

Natural Rights: 1928–48

Body-Soul Unity: 362–68, 382

Extraordinary Care: 2278–79

Euthanasia: 2276–79, 2324

CHAPTER 7

Critical Race Theory and Justice

*"And will not God vindicate his elect, who cry to him
day and night? Will he delay long over them? I tell you,
he will vindicate them speedily. Nevertheless, when the
Son of man comes, will he find faith on earth?"*

—Luke 18:7–8

Building a Foundation

Before we present the issue of critical race theory, it's essential
that we have a sense of virtue and some guiding principles
from the Church's social doctrine.

VIRTUE: *JUSTICE*
(SEE *CCC* 1807)

Justice is a high moral virtue. It is the duty to give to another
their due, whether in a punitive or positive sense. It involves
our obligation to give God His due as well as our neighbor. Justice requires a constant and firm will of heart. It disposes and
strengthens us to integrity and honesty. Justice compels us to
respect the rights of each person as well as the common good.

PRINCIPLE: *COMMON GOOD*
(SEE *CCC* 1905–12, 1924–27)

The common good is understood as the sum total of social conditions which allow people, either as groups or as individuals, to reach their fulfillment more fully and more easily. The common good concerns the life of each person. It calls for prudence from each, and even more from those who exercise an office of authority. It consists of three essential elements: respect for persons, social well-being and development, and peace as the stability and security of a just order.

A SECOND PRINCIPLE: *EQUALITY*
(SEE *CCC* 369–70, 1934–38)

As a social principle, equality teaches that men and women have been created with parallel dignity. Man and woman possess an inalienable dignity that comes to them immediately from God, their Creator. Man and woman are both with one and the same dignity "in the image of God." In their "being-man" and "being-woman," they reflect the Creator's wisdom and goodness. As such, the principle of equality argues against every form of social or cultural discrimination in fundamental personal rights on the grounds of sex, race, color, social conditions, language, or religion. These must be named and removed as incompatible with God's design.

Taking Our Stand

Since we have the assistance of virtue, and some principles from the Church's social doctrine, we are now ready to dive into the question of critical race theory.

"SOMETHING JUST ISN'T RIGHT."

Some time ago, a Catholic business professional reached out to me. He was a part of an apostolate where I had assisted as a chaplain earlier in my priesthood. The gentleman knew of my training in moral theology and asked if we could meet for lunch. I happened to be scheduled for a talk in his area and agreed to meet up.

When we met for lunch, the usually cheerful man seemed sullen and distracted. I wasn't sure what happened and feared something may have occurred in his family. As we passed through small talk, I realized something else was on his mind, and so I just asked him, "What's going on? It seems you have the weight of the world on your shoulders." The man looked at me and then started our real conversation.

"Father, I've always taken my faith seriously, and I've always treated people how I would want to be treated. I've never judged anyone on their race or any other personal aspect. I respect people. I've only ever assessed people on their job performance and abilities."

I wasn't sure what we were leading up to, and so I just listened.

"Well, Father, I'm being told that I'm a racist and that my company is systemically racist. I had to let someone go, and they were a minority. Their job performance was weak.

They were corrected and counseled for a couple of months with no change. After going through the process, I terminated their employment. Well, they got a lawyer, and now my company is in jeopardy. I documented everything, like I always do, and the facts should speak for themselves. But they're not."

He continued, "I'm declared a racist. And I'm shocked. I hate racism. I've worked for everything I have, and I want others to have that same chance, no matter what their skin color is. The things that are being said about me are shocking, Father. I'm having trouble sleeping. I would never judge someone by the color of their skin. I did everything right: I evaluated an employee, I gave them a chance to change, and when they didn't, I let them go. I've done this same process for over a decade. What's going on? *Something just isn't right.*"

Yes, something just isn't right!

The gentleman was a true business professional. He wasn't aware of the cultural movements of social engineering, identity politics, reverse discrimination, critical race theory, and cancel culture. He was a man who judged by job performance. He always relied on that standard to be the great equalizer. But our world has changed. Justice is under attack. Ideology has gone to extremes. Good people need to know what's happening and how they can reveal and counteract these divisive movements in our society.

With this in mind, we need to understand the virtue of justice, denounce any true racism, and be aware of ideologies and movements that usurp noble realities—such as racial equality—and use them for their own purposes which have nothing to do with the hijacked issue. In particular, we need to be aware of the historical foe of critical theory and its use in racial issues today.

Are we ready to dissect the critical race theory and reaffirm true justice? In our own lives, are we willing to take a stand for authentic justice? Are we willing to be called horrible names in order to expose the lies and exaggerations of ideologies in our day?

THE NOBLE VIRTUE OF JUSTICE

It is important that we have a clear and strong understanding and sense of justice. Justice is an essential virtue in a healthy society. Its absence or exaggeration can cause inequality, harm, and chaos. Simply put, justice is giving to another person what is his due. A person's "due" can be expressed in a positive manner—return a loaned item in as good a shape as it was when first borrowed—and in a punitive manner—a person must serve time in prison for an offense to a neighbor's dignity. In both ways, justice serves and builds up the common good. When exercised rightly, therefore, justice allows a society to flourish.

Building upon justice, a society legislates its laws and forms its policies. A society must ensure that its laws (and policies) are compliant with justice and that they facilitate a truly just and fair interaction between people under its care. If a law (or policy) undermines or offends justice, then it is rightly termed an "unjust" law.

Justice is focused on the care of persons, their dignity, and their rights and responsibilities. Justice is violated, therefore, when it is exercised indiscriminately. Collective guilt and punishment are an offense to justice. As a virtue, and a basis for law, justice evaluates specific people, actions, laws, and policies. There is no "broad brush" when it comes to justice.

Have I sought to fulfill the demands of justice in my own life? In my exercise of justice, do I respect the dignity of my neighbor? Have I ever violated the dignity and rights of someone by a use of corporate punishment?

> "Remove justice, and what are kingdoms but
> gangs of criminals on a large scale?"
>
> —Saint Augustine

CONTENT OF CHARACTER

Rather than succumbing to ideology or cultural movements, justice is called to be blind; it is not concerned with gender, race, or socio-economic status. It simply assesses human dignity, rights and responsibilities, and the "due" that is required to persons and to the common good.

In American history, this important lesson was summarized by the Protestant pastor and theologian Dr. Martin Luther King Jr. In his famous "I Have a Dream" speech, he dreamt of a day when his children would not be judged by the color of their skin but by the content of their character.

> "I have a dream that my four little children will
> one day live in a nation where they will not be
> judged by the color of their skin but by the con-
> tent of their character. I have a dream today."
>
> —Martin Luther King Jr., Speech at
> the Lincoln Memorial, 28 August 1963

Yes, justice is concerned about the content of character. It does not allow itself to be swayed by passion or preference, fear or favor. Justice, therefore, cannot be manipulated to support false race theories, reverse discrimination, identity politics, hyperbolic summaries of any race, misrepresentation of others based on the color of their skin, or destruction and violence toward anyone. In the course of human affairs, justice can be ignored and dismissed. But regardless of bad law, forced policy, or social pressure, justice will triumph in the course of time.

Do I labor to build up the content of my character? Do I base my judgments on the content of people's characters? Have I ever allowed other factors, such as race, to influence my moral judgements and/or my interactions with other people?

> "Justice is a certain rectitude of mind where-
> by a man does what he ought to do in the
> circumstances confronting him."
>
> —Saint Thomas Aquinas

The Scourge of Racism and Just Anger

As the critical race theory is unmasked, it is important that the topics of racism, racial harmony within society, and just anger be addressed and explained.

Racism is a scourge on society. It is the willful discrimination of a person or group of people based on their racial identity. It is a violation of justice. Racism is a grave affront to the dignity of the human person and to the rights and social acceptance that is their due. Racism presumes the inferiority of a racial group, isolates and belittles the targeted race, and refuses it the right ordering of justice within culture and society. Racism is the social philosophy that motivates the Ku Klux Klan, the neo-Nazis, and the Black Panthers, among many other groups.

Racism is a grave sin and has always been denounced within the Christian moral tradition. There is no room in the heart of a Christian disciple for the darkness of racism or of any other form of discrimination.

"The equality of men rests essentially on their dignity as persons and the rights that flow from it: Every form of social or cultural discrimination in fundamental personal rights on the grounds of sex, race, color, social conditions, language, or religion must be curbed and eradicated as incompatible with God's design."

—*Catechism of the Catholic Church*, no. 1935

As children of God, we are called to seek harmony with one another, to respect and learn from our racial and other differences as a people, and to labor for justice and peace within our society. Peace is the tranquility of order, and justice is an essential part of the order within society that ushers in and preserves true peace. As God's children, we are commissioned to be peacemakers. We are to sincerely welcome and accept others, cherishing and acknowledging their dignity, and be a source of human flourishing and growth within society and culture.

Wherever and whenever racism is found in people, laws, policies, or actions, it must be confronted, denounced, and stripped of any pretend credibility. People of goodwill rightly express a just anger over racism. Such anger is to be properly ordered by justice, however, and expressed in a way that is both civil and civilizing.

Have I ever shown discrimination to another person because of his race? Do I confront and fight against racism whenever or wherever it's found in society and culture? Do I allow justice to properly order any just anger in my heart?

"No one heals himself by wounding another."

—Saint Ambrose

"He who is not angry when there is just cause for anger is immoral. Why? Because anger looks to the good of justice. And if you can live amid injustice without anger, you are immoral as well as unjust."

—Saint Thomas Aquinas

Unjust Laws and Racist Acts

There are times in which a society legislates and enacts certain unjust laws. An unjust law is one that betrays human dignity and the virtue of justice. Although unjust laws are actual laws, with the possibility of punishment or penalties attached to them, they must, nonetheless, be civilly disobeyed. Such laws must be exposed, rallied against in the forum of public opinion, sought to be peacefully overturned by the political process, and even civilly disobeyed. People of goodwill cannot become accomplices to unjust laws.

If a law is racist, it is unjust and must be overturned. If a law empowers discrimination—or any unfair treatment of any persons—it is an unjust law and must be changed. There is no moral concession or possibility of compromise in the face of such injustice. A society is only truly civilized to the extent that its laws and justice system reflect justice— namely, that it contains just laws that are equally applied to all. Christians are bound to pursue a truly civilized society that celebrates justice and seeks to give to each person what is truly their due.

Have I sought justice in all my actions? Do I fight for justice in the public forum and rally against unjust laws? Have I remained quiet in the face of evil and injustice?

"How does one determine whether a law is just or unjust? A just law is a man-made code that squares with the moral law or the law of God. An unjust law is a code that is out of harmony with the moral law. To put it in the terms of St. Thomas Aquinas: An unjust law is a human law that is not rooted in eternal law and natural law. Any law that uplifts human personality is just. Any law that degrades human personality is unjust."

—Martin Luther King Jr., *Letter from a Birmingham Jail*, 16 April 1963

CRITICAL THEORY AND SOCIAL UPHEAVAL

In understanding the noble virtue of justice, we rightly denounce any form of racism. We identify the reality of unjust laws, such as laws that protect or empower racism, and peacefully call for their repeal. Whenever and wherever there is racism, it must be identified and denounced.

All of these statements are in harmony with the Christian moral tradition. Yet none of them are within the critical race theory. In fact, such statements would be falsely called racist themselves. Such irrationality reflects the ideological and extremist views of the critical race theory.

Some history and context might help us. The critical theory, which can be applied to anything from socioeconomic groups, to gender, to race, to sexual orientation, and more, was drafted and became very popular at the beginning of the twentieth century. The theory claims that people are solely defined by the specified attribute in question. The theory argues that their entire dignity is exclusively bound up in this one attribute of their total personhood.

The critical theory provokes the people of the designated attribute. It tells them that they are victims and are being oppressed by everyone outside of their group. Anyone not in the specified victim group is either an aggressor or an advocate. The theory purposely fans flames of emotional anger and misguided resentment. It continues by telling the victim group that they can only be truly free by overturning the entire social structure that the theory claims is oppressing them.

In our day, the critical theory is focused on race. The critical race theory tells people that they are only identified— they are only truly persons—by the color of their skin. It claims that everyone who is not a part of their racial group, or any institution that was not founded by members of this racial group, is inherently racist and oppressive and must be brought down.

The critical race theory tells people that simply because they are not a member of a specific racial group, they are *de facto* racists. As such, the theory is unjust since justice is blind and must make its decisions based on actions, policies, laws, and states of affairs. The critical race theory leads to reverse discrimination and social tension. The theory violates justice by inversing it and falsely applying it in a collective manner. As such, the critical race theory is the theory that is behind the injustice of supposed "systemic racism." It is the theory that supports and motivates Black Lives Matter, Inc. and Antifa.

The critical theory is a school of thought that is purposely designed to cause social tension and weaken free societies, democratic governments, and organized religion. It is facilitated in such a way so as to provide a forum for ideology, socialism, and the raw exercise of a freedom unrestrained by truth or principles of moral goodness. In this context, the critical theory is an evil system of thought that must be confronted and peacefully opposed by Christians and all people of goodwill.

Do I avoid irrational anger and false resentment in my life? Do I seek to follow the reasonable guidance of justice? Do I refuse to be mastered by false ideologies?

"Most men seem to live according to sense, rather than reason."

—Saint Thomas Aquinas

DENOUNCING THE CRITICAL THEORY

There can be no mistake, as Christians, we are opposed to the critical theory and its current application of the critical race theory. In justice, we cannot accept its false claim of systemic racism since justice demands that we judge specific actions, policies, and laws. We do not look at the color of a person's skin in determining fault or moral failing. Rather, we look to the content of their character. We do not paint broadly with a wide brush, misapplying justice in a collective manner.

As Christians, if and when there is racism, we confront it. We seek to overturn any expression of racism. We do not, however, unjustly claim that an entire society, political system, culture, set of laws, or anyone outside of a specific group is racist. We deal with specific people and states of affairs as justice demands.

As Catholic Christians, we should be particularly cautious of the critical theory since it is a theory grounded in a philosophy that wages war against organized religion, and specifically against the Roman Catholic Church. Simply put, the critical theory is evil and a clear violation of true justice and we must be vehemently opposed to it.

Do I understand the inherent moral flaws of the critical theory? Do I expose their faults to my neighbors and argue for true justice in our society? Do I understand the violation of justice when it is falsely applied in a collective manner?

"To bear with patience wrongs done to oneself is a mark of perfection, but to bear with patience wrongs done to someone else is a mark of imperfection and even of actual sin."

—Saint Thomas Aquinas

JUSTICE IN THE TRENCHES

The question of the critical race theory requires a solid understanding of justice, which is the duty of giving to another his due, whether in a punitive or positive sense. Justice compels us to respect the rights of each person, as well as the common good. It relies on other virtues, such as integrity and fortitude. Justice is called to be "blind" and to make its judgments based on moral truth rather than on a person's personal aspects or traits.

Justice cannot be applied in a collective manner since such an application would offend the dignity and fairness of the multiple people involved in such a summary judgment. In this way, and in several others, justice opposes the critical race theory. In addition, justice dismisses any other such ideology that relies on collective judgment, social engineering, identity politics, reverse discrimination, and cancel culture since these violate a person's due to fair judgment of their specific character or of a set of circumstances.

Key Takeaways

As a quick reference, here are the key takeaways on the critical race theory and justice:

- Justice is the giving to another person what is their due. It is focused on human dignity, rights, and responsibilities.
- Justice has both a punitive and positive expression. Both are essential in a healthy society.
- Laws and public policies are "just" to the degree that they reflect justice.
- Justice focuses on specific people, actions, laws, and policies.
- Justice cannot be exercised in a collective way. Such a use of justice is an abuse of the virtue and its power.
- Justice is called to be blind. It focuses on the content

of one's character rather than on the traits of a person, such as race, gender, or socioeconomic status.

- Racism is the willful discrimination of a person or group of people based on their racial identity. It is a grave evil and an affront to justice.
- Christian believers and people of goodwill are called to be peacemakers and to seek harmony in society.
- Laws that violate justice and betray human dignity are "unjust" and must be fought against and civilly disobeyed.
- The critical race theory violates justice by its identity politics, reverse discrimination, and its collective assertion of systemic racism. The theory fuels social upheaval and is opposed to democratic government and organized religion.

Going to the Mountain

Having presented our arguments, and always seeking to speak the truth in love, we now retreat and go to the mountain for prayer, spiritual rejuvenation, and supplication.

Prayer

Eternal Father,
We turn to You.
We trust You. We adore You.
You have created us in Your own image.
You have blessed us,
and made us brothers and sisters to one another.
Guide us with Your Spirit.

Teach us to love.

Help us to show justice to one another.

Grant us the grace of humility.

Father,

Show us Your way of love.

Cast out all spirits of hatred or injustice.

Fill us with Your goodness.

Strengthen us in Your kindness.

Grant us Your peace!

Through Christ Our Lord.

Amen.

EXAMINATION OF CONSCIENCE

The following questions are given as help to examine our consciences on the issue of the critical race theory and justice:

- Have I always given to God what is His due? Do I rely on His grace?
- Have I shown justice to my neighbor by speech and actions?
- Have I always justly compensated others for their work or labors?
- Have I defended others when they have been treated unjustly?
- Do I ever falsely apply justice in a collective way?
- Is my exercise of justice blind? Do I treat all people equally?
- Have I been racist in my interaction with any other person?
- Do I denounce racism in any form?

- Do I publicly oppose any theory or view that violates justice?
- Do I see God's image in each of my neighbors?

Based on the insights of this examination of conscience, you're encouraged to go and make a good confession.

After reviewing this social issue, recommit yourself to the Lordship of Jesus Christ and ask for the intercession of your guardian angel.

"Suscipe" Prayer

Take, Lord, and receive all my liberty,
my memory, my understanding,
and my entire will,
All I have and call my own.

You have given all to me.
To You, Lord, I return it.

Everything is Yours; do with it what You will.
Give me only Your love and Your grace,
that is enough for me.
Amen.

Guardian Angel Prayer

Angel of God,
My guardian dear,
To whom God's love
Commits me here.
Ever this day,
Be at my side,

To light and guard
To rule and guide.
Amen.

Added Devotional

A suggested devotional: Pray the Glorious Mysteries of the Rosary, especially the third mystery: the descent of the Holy Spirit upon the apostles and Our Lady. In your prayer, focus on the power of the Holy Spirit to make us wise and to renew the face of the earth. Ask for the grace to see God's image in every human person. Ask Him to remove all forms of racism from our world and to bless us with true justice and peace.

Suggested saintly intercessors: Saint Martin de Porres, Saint Katharine Drexel, Saint Josephine Bakhita, Saint Peter Claver, Blessed Francisco de Paula Victor, Blessed Isidore Bakanja, Blessed Emilian Kovch, and Venerable Henriette Delille.

"All the efforts of the human mind cannot exhaust the essence of a single fly." (In other words, human ideologies and theories can never fully grasp the complexity of real being.)

—Saint Thomas Aquinas

"Beware of the person of one book." (In other words, avoid people who have only one view, since it oftentimes becomes absolutized and dangerous.)"

—Saint Thomas Aquinas

CITATIONS FROM THE
CATECHISM OF THE CATHOLIC CHURCH

Justice: 1807
Common Good: 1905–12, 1924–27
Equality: 369–70, 1934–38
Discrimination: 1935
Human Dignity: 27, 306, 308, 356–57, 364, 369, 872, 1004, 1700–15, 1730, 1929–30, 1934, 2158, 2203, 2334
Natural Rights: 1928–48
Solidarity: 1939–42
Human Respect: 2407–18
Social Justice: 2426–36

Chapter 8

The Male Priesthood and Gender Equality

"In these days he went out into the hills to pray; and all night he continued in prayer to God. And when it was day, he called his disciples, and chose from them twelve, whom he named apostles."

—*Luke 6:12–13*

Building a Foundation

Before we present the issue of a male priesthood and gender equality, it's essential that we have a sense of virtue and some guiding principles from the Church's social doctrine.

VIRTUE: *FAITH*
(SEE *CCC* 1814–16)

Faith is one of the core Christian virtues. It gives us the grace to believe in God, His revelation, and His words and deeds. By faith, the human person is able to commit his entire self to God. As such, faith requires works, such as service to the poor and sick. Without works, faith is dead.

PRINCIPLE: *COMPLEMENTARITY*
(SEE *CCC* 2331–36)

Complementarity is the principle that illustrates the unique and harmonious relationship between man and woman. God created men and women in His own image and placed within them the vocation, capacity, and responsibility of love and communion. Complementarity affects the entire person, body and soul. It demonstrates that our bodies—united to our innermost being—are not accidents that can be manipulated. Our bodies and souls are one. The male person has been formed to match and complete the female person, and vice versa. And so, the nuptial friendship is a particular friendship between one man and one woman for life.

A SECOND PRINCIPLE: *HUMAN DIGNITY*
(SEE *CCC* 27, 306, 308, 356–57, 364, 369, 872, 1004, 1700–15, 1730, 1929–30, 1934, 2158, 2203, 2334)

The principle of human dignity asserts that every human person is made in the image of God. Human dignity shows that every human being is a *someone*, not a *something*. As such, every human person has the power to act on their own and is capable of self-knowledge, of self-possession, and of freely giving himself and entering into communion with other persons. Human dignity upholds that the human person is an intelligent and free cause who, by knowledge and love, can share in God's own life. While such dignity can regrettably be eclipsed and offended, it cannot be taken away by any created entity, including the person himself.

Taking Our Stand

Since we have the assistance of virtue, and some principles from the Church's social doctrine, we are now ready to dive into the question of a male priesthood and gender equality.

"WE DIDN'T WANT TO GO TO HELL."

Some years ago, when the Church was blessed and enriched by the conversion of former Anglican and Episcopalian priests into the fullness of faith, I heard a powerful story about the Church's teachings on a male-only priesthood. In the various groups of converts, there were some former female priests. In their conversion into the Catholic Church, they had to denounce their supposed Holy Order and accept the entirety of the Church's teachings. Each of these women did so without question or hesitation.

After the process, some of these women were at an event with some liberal women religious. The conversation was as intriguing as it was provocative. It was clear that the sisters were confounded by the story of these other women since, in many respects, they had achieved everything that the liberal sisters had ever wanted, and yet, they denounced it all. It was shocking, almost offensive to the sisters. The discussion led to some interesting biblical truths and acts of faith.

The sisters asked multiple questions about the women's former priestly ministries, their process of discernment into the Catholic Church, and their denunciation of their sup-posed order. The conversation began to go in circles, and it became clear that there was one obvious unasked question in the entire exchange. Finally, one of the older sisters just asked,

"Why? Why would you do that? You had the priesthood and you left it? Why would you do that?" The tone of the inquiry was charged with a sense of frustration and betrayal.

One of the new converts smiled gently and then unleashed her full biblical scholarship on the subject (some of which we will get into shortly). When she was done, she concluded, "And so, Sister, it became clear to us from revelation that God has not called women to the ministerial priesthood. Having that knowledge, we couldn't disobey God's will. We didn't want to go to hell. And so we denounced what was not of God and sought entrance in the fullness of faith."

The sisters didn't know how to respond. Here were highly theologically educated women who "had it all" and were willing to leave everything so that they could more perfectly follow the Lord Jesus. The liberal sisters were humbled into silence by such faith and docility. Meanwhile, the new Catholic women continued their conversation with all the grace and joy that comes with having the fullness of faith.

In our discipleship, do we appreciate the wisdom contained in the teachings of the Church? Do we show humility and obedience before biblical truths? Are we willing to give up everything in order to follow the teachings of the Lord Jesus and His Church?

The Last Good Ole Boys' Club?

Due to poor teaching on the topic of a male-only priesthood, there are many believers who misunderstand the Church's doctrine on this matter. There are some who have applied a misplaced notion of justice to the topic and have therefore assumed that the Church is engaged in some form of sexist injustice toward women. As one dismissive believer coined it, "The Catholic priesthood is the last good ole boys' club." Or as a recent activist wrongly concluded, "Women only have six sacraments in the Catholic Church." Of course, the implication of such a slogan is that since women cannot be ordained, somehow the sacrament of Holy Orders is not a sacrament for them.

It's regrettable that some have these mistaken understandings of why the Church can only ordain men to the priesthood. In truth, there are actually some very sound anthropological, biblical, and doctrinal reasons as to why the Church cannot ordain women to the ministerial priesthood. Before diving into those, it's important that we address the question of whether or not the Church is engaged in some form of injustice against women.

In my life, do I seek the Church's answers to my questions or do I allow our culture to falsely teach me about truth? When I find an issue that challenges me, do I approach the Church's teachings with docility or defiance? Do I welcome the Church as both my mother and teacher?

"Wherefore, in order that all doubt may be removed regarding a matter of great importance, a matter which pertains to the Church's divine constitution itself, in virtue of my ministry of confirming the brethren (cf. Lk 22:32), I declare that the Church has no authority whatsoever to confer priestly ordination on women and that this judgment is to be definitively held by all the Church's faithful."

—Pope Saint John Paul II, apostolic letter
Ordinatio Sacerdotalis, no. 4

A QUESTION OF JUSTICE?

Justice is a powerful and noble virtue. When it's invoked, it must be used well. Our tradition defines justice as giving someone their due. An injustice is committed when someone is due something but it is not given to them. In terms of the ministerial priesthood, no one is "due" an ordination to such sacred service. No one is entitled to it, no one can demand it, and no one can rightly expect it. Rather, the priesthood is a gift. Therefore, any appeal to justice is misplaced in this context.

The call to the priesthood is given by God through the mediation and discernment of the Church. It is based upon God's revelation, as contained in Sacred Scripture and Sacred Tradition and as interpreted and applied by the Magisterium (the formal teaching office) of the Church under the guidance of the Holy Spirit.

The Church and the Holy Spirit have discerned and directed, based on the life and ministry of the Lord Jesus, that the Lord has reserved his priesthood to men and has not called women to serve Him in this particular way. While there are abundant other ways in which women are called to serve the Lord (and should do so), the ministerial priesthood is not one of them.

As Saint Paul reminds us, we are one body, but of many parts: "Now there are varieties of gifts, but the same Spirit; and there are varieties of services, but the same Lord; and there are varieties of working, but it is the same God who inspires them all in every one. To each is given the manifestation of the Spirit for the common good" (1 Cor 12:4–7). This can be a hard teaching in a culture that has merged equality and complementarity, that has dismissed the rule of faith and the movement of the Holy Spirit, and that has regularly misapplied justice to issues where it has no competency.

This teaching is further made difficult by the authentic sexism and injustice that is sometimes found among specific leaders within the Church. Deceptively, the Church's broader teaching on a male-only priesthood can be manipulated and used as a shield or defense of such sinful actions and policies. Any such sexism in the Church must be rightly identified and denounced. We must be careful, however, not to associate sound doctrine with the sinful actions or policies of some.

In spite of the challenges, the truth is consistent and harmonious. This chapter, therefore, will develop and explain the teaching about a male-only priesthood. It will provide the anthropological, biblical, and doctrinal reasons behind such a teaching.

Ask yourself: Will I have an open heart to hear what the Church and the Holy Spirit are teaching? Do I struggle to understand the proper place of justice in the issues of our day? Do I understand that women have an important role in the life of the Church even though they are not called to the ministerial priesthood?

"Moreover, and above all, to consider the ministerial priesthood as a human right would be to misjudge it's nature completely: baptism does not confer any personal title to public ministry within the Church. The priesthood is not conferred for the honor or advantage of the recipient, but for the service of God and the Church; it is the object of a specific and totally gratuitous vocation: 'You did not choose me, no, I chose you; and I commissioned you . . .' (Jn. 15:16; Heb. 5:4)."

—Congregation for the Doctrine of the Faith,
instruction *Inter Insigniores*, no. 6

ANTHROPOLOGICALLY, A MALE PRIESTHOOD

All human beings, male and female, are made in God's image (see Gn 1:27). Both genders, therefore, share an equality of dignity. There is no subordinate gender. The two were created so as to wonderfully reflect God's beauty, majesty, and perfection. As such, the genders are complementary. There is a harmonious interaction between them. Their spiritual and biological matrix match each other. From this basic and observable anthropological truth, other truths can be drawn. In particular, the complementarity of the two genders displays for us that, while the genders are equal in dignity, they are in fact quite different. They are not the same. Equality does not mean uniformity.

"It therefore remains for us to meditate more deeply on the nature of the real equality of the baptized which is one of the great affirmations of Christianity; equality is in no way identity, for the Church is a differentiated body, in which each individual has his or her role. The roles are distinct, and must not be confused; they do not favor the superiority of some vis-a-vis the others, nor do they provide an excuse for jealousy; the only better gift, which can and must be desired, is love (1 Cor 12–13). The greatest in the Kingdom of Heaven are not the ministers but the saints."

—Congregation for the Doctrine of the Faith,
instruction *Inter Insigniores*, no. 6

Each gender contains its own "genius." It possesses its own bodily, spiritual, emotional, intellectual, and sense awareness. Each gender comes with a natural set of gifts, abilities, and inclinations. While cultural contexts can sometimes complicate this discernment of gifts between the genders, the difference ultimately shines out in spite of cultural situations (or social engineering meant to diminish or blur them).

The genius of each gender must be honored and celebrated. The Church has always shown great deference to the genius of both men and women. The vocation of marriage, the family, society, and the very structure of the Church relies mutually upon the genius of both genders and the dynamic relationship that should exist between them. In this spirit, one theologian remarked, "The motherhood of the Church depends upon the fatherhood of her priests."

Do I appreciate the difference between the genders? Do I revere the genius of my own gender? Do I show respect and honor to the genius of the other gender?

"The Church gives thanks *for all the manifestations of the feminine 'genius'* which have appeared in the course of history, in the midst of all peoples and nations; she gives thanks for all the charisms which the Holy Spirit distributes to women in the history of the People of God, for all the victories which she owes to their faith, hope and charity: she gives thanks for all *the fruits of feminine holiness.*"

—Pope Saint John Paul II, apostolic letter
Mulieris Dignitatem, no. 31

In recognizing the genius of the two genders, the Church acknowledges the importance of the male gender in the priesthood. In discerning the human nature of the Lord Jesus, and His own identity as a male within the human race, it becomes clear that the masculine genius was chosen by God for the priestly ministry. Since the Church teaches that a priest acts *in persona Christi*—in the person of Christ—it follows that priests must also be of the male gender.

Moreover, in the Lord Jesus's selection of the apostles, the Church further discerns a male-only priesthood, since the Lord—who was not bound by cultural norms in any other aspect of His ministry—chose only men for His priesthood after a night of prayer and communion with the Father. While the anthropological reason cannot be used as a strictly apologetical reason, it nonetheless does provide a broader human reason as to why only men are called to the priesthood.

Do I appreciate the genius of the different genders? Do I value the masculinity of the Lord Jesus and of my local priests? Do I respect the spiritual fatherhood of my priests?

"The same natural resemblance is required for persons as for things: when Christ's role in the Eucharist is to be expressed sacramentally, there would not be this 'natural resemblance' which must exist between Christ and his minister if the role of Christ were not taken by a man: in such a case it would be difficult to see in the minister the image of Christ. For Christ himself was and remains a man."

—Congregation for the Doctrine of the Faith, instruction *Inter Insigniores*, no. 5

Biblically, A Male Priesthood

As already pointed out, the Lord Jesus did not call women to the group of apostles (see Lk 6:12–13). The attempt to dismiss this point by citing the "cultural milieu" of the Lord's times is unbiblical. The Lord's approach to women was very different and countercultural for His day. He oftentimes intentionally and purposely broke with the expectations and customs of His age.

As cited in the instruction *Inter Insigniores* of the Congregation for the Doctrine of the Faith (2), the Lord Jesus oftentimes astonished His disciples by His interaction with women. For example, when He conversed publicly with the Samaritan woman (see Jn 4:27), when He takes no notice of the state of legal impurity of the woman who had suffered from hemorrhages (see Mt 9:20), when He allows a sinful woman to approach Him in the house of Simon the Pharisee (see Lk 7:37), and by pardoning the woman taken in adultery, He means to show that one must not be more severe towards the fault of a woman than towards that of a man (see Jn 8:11). The Lord does not hesitate to depart from the Mosaic Law in order to affirm the equality of the rights and duties of men and women with regard to the marriage bond (see Mk 10:2; Mt 19:3).

The instruction of the Congregation for the Doctrine of the Faith continues: In the Lord's itinerant ministry, He was accompanied not only by the twelve but also by a group of women (see Lk 8:2). Contrary to the Jewish mentality, which did not give great value to the testimony of women, it was women who were chosen to be the first witnesses of the risen Lord, and it was they who were sent by the Lord Jesus to take the first paschal message to the apostles (see Mt 28:7; Lk 24:9; Jn 20:11) in order to prepare them to become the official witnesses to the Resurrection.

And yet, even as He chose to break with many of the customs and gender roles of His day, the Lord Jesus still did not choose women to be in the ordained ministry. As developed in the instruction of the Congregation for the Doctrine of the Faith (3), the early Church continued the practice set by the Lord Jesus. On the day of Pentecost, the Holy Spirit came upon all the disciples, men and women (see Acts 2:1; 1:14), but the call to preach was only given to Peter and the eleven (see Acts 2:14).

As the Church, especially through the ministry of Saint Paul, went beyond the realm of Jewish Christianity and began to engage the gentile cultures (which were accustomed to female priests), the question of women's ordination could have been raised. And yet, no such inquiry was brought forward within the Christian community due to its regard and fidelity to the practice of the Lord.

In fact, the Acts of the Apostles and the letters of Saint Paul show that certain women worked alongside Saint Paul for the sake of the Gospel (see Rom 16:3–12; Phil 4:3). In addition, some of them even exercised important ministries. These included Priscilla, who took it upon herself to complete the instruction of Apollos (see Acts 18:26), Phoebe, in service to the Church of Cenchreae (see Rom 16:1), and Lydia, who is the first recorded convert to Christianity in Europe and was a businesswoman devoted to Saint Paul (see Acts 16:14–15).

And yet, even with all these ministries and roles in play, there was never a question of whether these women should be ordained. The biblical narrative is consistent and undimmed. The Lord Jesus did not choose women for the priestly ministry. Later, even as many other ministries and apostolates were entrusted to women in the early Church, the priesthood was clearly not one of them.

Do I accept the biblical testimony of the priesthood? Do I understand the important work that women have in the life of the Church? Do I seek to fulfill my part in the mandate of the Gospel?

"As we have seen, an examination of the Gospels shows on the contrary that Jesus broke with the prejudices of his time, by widely contravening the discriminations practiced with regard to women. One therefore cannot maintain that, by not calling women to enter the group of the Apostles, Jesus was simply letting himself be guided by reasons of expediency. For all the more reason, social and cultural conditioning did not hold back the Apostles working in the Greek milieu, where the same forms of discrimination did not exist."

—Congregation for the Doctrine of the Faith,
instruction *Inter Insigniores*, no. 4

The Church's Proper Focus

In the Church's esteem for the ministerial priesthood, she places it within the context of holiness and keeps her proper focus on sainthood. While the priesthood is a cherished gift within the life of the Church, it also is in service to the universal call to holiness.

In the doctrinal explanation of the male-only priesthood presented in this chapter, it is important to know the mind and heart of the Church not simply in terms of orthodox teaching but also in terms of her call for all the baptized to become saints.

In contrast to the disobedience, dismissiveness, and smugness of some theologians who pride themselves in waging battles that cause confusion and anxiety among the faithful, the Church responds with kindness, clarity, and the perennial call to seek the face of God in and above all things.

Do I pursue holiness in my state in life? Do I engage in battles against Church doctrine? Do I seek unity among all believers as we mutually seek holiness in our lives?

"Moreover, it is to the holiness of the faithful that the hierarchical structure of the Church is totally ordered. For this reason, the Declaration *Inter Insigniores* recalls: 'the only better gift, which can and must be desired, is love (cf. 1 Cor 12 and 13). The greatest in the Kingdom of Heaven are not the ministers but the saints.'"

—Pope Saint John Paul II, apostolic letter
Ordinatio Sacerdotalis, no. 3

OUR LADY, QUEEN OF THE APOSTLES

In speaking of holiness in the life of the Church, there is no one within the fallen human race who was graced more or raised to a higher height of holiness than Mary of Nazareth. Chosen by God the Father, she became the Mother of God and the first disciple of the Lord Jesus. Spouse of the Spirit, she is the mother of all believers.

After the Lord's ascension, as the apostles waited for the coming of the Holy Spirit in the upper room, Mary joined the apostolic community (see Acts 1:14). With the apostles, she received the Holy Spirit. Our Lady did not receive the Holy Spirit for priesthood but for her own vocation as Queen of the Apostles and Mother of the Church. When the apostles, therefore, were called to find a successor for Judas, they turned to the male disciples in their number (see Acts 1:15–26). If ever a woman were called by God to the priesthood, it would have been Mary. And yet, she was not called and didn't expect to be called to the priestly ministry.

Mary stands as a breathing validation that the Lord Jesus has not called women to the priesthood. Although there is much work to be done by all the members of the Church, male and female, the priestly ministry has clearly been reserved to men.

The instruction of the Congregation for the Doctrine of the Faith (2) quotes Pope Innocent III, who wrote, "Although the Blessed Virgin Mary surpassed in dignity and in excellence all the Apostles, nevertheless it was not to her but to them that the Lord entrusted the keys of the Kingdom of Heaven."

Do I honor Mary as the Queen of Apostles and Mother of the Church? Do I show her true homage as she fulfills her vocation throughout time? Do I accept and live according to God's will in my life?

"Furthermore, the fact that the Blessed Virgin Mary, Mother of God and Mother of the Church, received neither the mission proper to the Apostles nor the ministerial priesthood clearly shows that the non-admission of women to priestly ordination cannot mean that women are of lesser dignity, nor can it be construed as discrimination against them. Rather, it is to be seen as the faithful observance of a plan to be ascribed to the wisdom of the Lord of the universe."

—Pope Saint John Paul II, apostolic letter
Ordinatio Sacerdotalis, no. 3

Faith in the Trenches

The question of a male priesthood and gender equality requires us to exercise the virtue of faith. Faith gives us the grace of God's revelation. It builds up our reason. Faith helps us to know our human nature, the two genders within our nature, and the complementarity between them. Faith shows us the proper exercise of justice. It helps us to know what is due, or not due, to our neighbors.

By faith, we are able to commit ourselves entirely to God. With faith, we can understand what and how certain supernatural gifts, such as the priesthood, are given by God to humanity. We can accept the divine will in the dispensation of His gifts. In this way, faith requires works. It calls for an act of surrender and trust.

Key Takeaways

As a quick reference, here are the key takeaways on a male priesthood and gender equality:

- The virtue of justice is giving to another what is his due. Justice does not pertain to the question of the ministerial priesthood since no one is entitled to it or has a right to it.

- The priesthood is a supernatural gift from God, who has chosen to bestow it on men.
- The Church is the one Body of Christ, but it is made up of many members with different functions and ministries. Men and women are called to ministry in the Church.
- Sexism is a grave violation of the moral law. It is to be identified and rooted out wherever it truly exists.
- All human beings, male and female, share an equality of dignity.
- The two genders within our human nature possess a complementarity. This complementarity shows us that our equality is not uniformity. The genders are equal but different.
- Each gender possesses a genius. God has chosen the masculine genius for the ministerial priesthood.
- The Lord Jesus chose only men for His priesthood.
- The early Church followed the Lord's example and called only men to the priestly ministry.
- Mary received the Holy Spirit with the apostles but was not called—not expected to be called—to the priesthood. Of all women, she was the most qualified to be a priest, and yet she was not called.

Going to the Mountain

Having presented our arguments, and always seeking to speak the truth in love, we now retreat and go to the mountain for prayer, spiritual rejuvenation, and supplication.

Prayer

Heavenly Father,
You are the Creator of all men and women.
You are our spiritual worship,
We turn to You.
Show us Your Face.
Help us to accept Your will,
As You bless us and dispense your gifts.
Father,
Grant us docility and openness.
Guide us to accept Your plan.
Remove any obstinacy from our hearts.
We surrender everything to You.
We follow You.
We love You.
We adore You.
Through Christ Our Lord.
Amen.

Examination of Conscience

The following questions are given as help to examine our consciences on the issue of a male priesthood and gender equality:

- Do I understand the complementarity of men and women?
- Do I value the masculine genius in the priesthood?
- Do I realize that the priesthood is a gift, not an entitlement or right?
- Do I pray for the men who are called to be priests?

- Do I avoid all forms of authentic sexism or discrimination?
- Do I welcome the genius and contribution of women in society and the Church?
- Have I defended the Church's teaching on a male-only priesthood?
- Do I value the vocation of Our Lady as Queen of Apostles and Mother of the Church?
- Do I support my local priests?
- Do I seek to faithfully live out my own vocation?

Based on the insights of this examination of conscience, you're encouraged to go and make a good confession.

After reviewing this social issue, recommit yourself to the Lordship of Jesus Christ and ask for the protection of your guardian angel.

"Suscipe" Prayer

Take, Lord, and receive all my liberty,
my memory, my understanding,
and my entire will,
All I have and call my own.

You have given all to me.
To You, Lord, I return it.

Everything is Yours; do with it what You will.
Give me only Your love and Your grace,
that is enough for me.
Amen.

GUARDIAN ANGEL PRAYER

Angel of God,
My guardian dear,
To whom God's love
Commits me here.
Ever this day,
Be at my side,
To light and guard
To rule and guide.
Amen.

ADDED DEVOTIONAL

A suggested devotional: Pray the Luminous Mysteries of the Rosary, especially the fifth mystery: the institution of the Eucharist. In your prayer, focus on the priesthood of Our Lord. Give thanks to God for the men who are called to the priesthood and for the gift of the Eucharist that comes to us through their hands. Pray for an end to authentic sexism and for a broader understanding of the Church's teachings on a male-only priesthood.

A suggested devotional: Pray the Stations of the Cross, especially the eleventh station: Jesus is nailed to the cross. In your prayer, ask God to bless our priests. Pray for a deepening of faith and love for the masculine genius in the priesthood.

Suggested saintly intercessors: Saint John Marie Vianney, Saint Therese the Little Flower, Saint John Bosco, Saint Pio of Pietrelcino, Saint John of Nepomuk, Saint Maximilian Kolbe, Saint Teresa of Avila, Saint Clare of Assisi, and Blessed Clemens August Graf von Galen.

"The priesthood is the love of the heart of Jesus. When
you see a priest, think of our Lord Jesus Christ."

—Saint John Marie Vianney

"Heavenly Father, grant that our priests be strengthened
and healed
by the power of the Eucharist they celebrate.
May the Word they proclaim give
them courage and wisdom.

We pray that all those whom they seek to serve
May see in them the love and care of Jesus,
Our Eternal High Priest, who is Lord for ever and ever.
Amen."

—Saint Faustina's Prayer for Priests

CITATIONS FROM THE
CATECHISM OF THE CATHOLIC CHURCH

Faith: 1814–16
Complementarity: 2331–36
Human Dignity: 27, 306, 308, 356–57, 364, 369, 872, 1004,
1700–15, 1730, 1929–30; 1934, 2158, 2203, 2334
Justice: 1807
Priesthood: 1544–53, 1562–68
Male Priesthood: 1577–78
Mary: 963–75

Conclusion

"They All Work Together!"

It's surprising how many Catholics are not aware of the depth of the Church's teachings and how readily available they are in the *Catechism of the Catholic Church*. Early in my priesthood, a medical doctor asked me for guidance. He wanted to go deeper in his faith and grow in his discipleship. He was a busy person, and so I suggested that he make a weekly Holy Hour and read the *Catechism* during the time of prayer. He was open to the idea and moved forward.

After a couple of months, he asked to see me for a follow up. When we met, he described the growth in his prayer. The weekly Holy Hour eventually led him to a daily decade of the Rosary, which led to him coming early to Mass to read the readings and spiritually prepare. As he was talking, I could see his new zeal for the spiritual life.

After describing his life of prayer, the gentleman became particularly excited. He sat up in his chair, raised his voice a little, and was really on fire as he spoke about the *Catechism of the Catholic Church*. He told me how inspired he was by the Church's teachings, saying, "They're so consistent. All of the teachings flow. They all work together!" He explained how he would flip from the portion of the *Catechism* on the Creed to the portion on the Christian way of life. In the process, he saw the inner harmony and dynamism of the Church's teachings. He was able to witness how our way of life flows from our way of belief. The life of a believer is one consecrated to Jesus Christ and lived out in fidelity to His teachings and those of His Church.

It is the Church's hope that every believer will encounter the Lord Jesus and, in this encounter, come to see the interior consistency of the Church's teachings as a help in knowing who Jesus is and how we are called to live as His disciples.

Ask yourself: Do I work on my spiritual life and desire to encounter the Lord Jesus? Do I study and work to know the Church's teachings? Do I show an obedience of faith and an active docility to these teachings?

> "If you don't behave as you believe, you
> will end by believing as you behave."
>
> —Venerable Fulton Sheen

What We've Learned

As a help in the process of encountering the Lord Jesus, this book has presented some of the social questions of our day in the light of the clear teachings of the Lord Jesus and His Church. The explanations in this book have attempted to cover all the areas of the related issues. It has sought to avoid nothing and to give a concise and thorough explanation of what the Lord and His Church teach. For believers and people of goodwill, these teachings present a way of life. They show us how we are called to live and how we can address the questions of our age.

The social issues that were selected were chosen because of the frequency of requests for pastoral guidance, their pressing importance, and their connection to movements that seek to change our society and moral understanding.

By learning divine wisdom and how we can respond to these issues, it's the perennial hope of the Church that we will speak—always in love—with conviction and boldness. Our fallen world needs the truth of the Gospel. It needs the light of the teachings of the Lord Jesus and His Church. These teachings have been given to us and we are called to live them, speak them, share them, and defend them.

Have I surrendered my life to the Lord Jesus and seek to live always by His Gospel? Do I realize my call to speak the truth in love? Do I defend what is true and good?

"I do not fear at all what men can do to me for speaking the truth. I only fear what God would do if I were to lie."

—Saint John Bosco

Our Mission Today

As Catholics, who hold the fullness of the faith, we are summoned out of our laziness, comfort, and desire for respectability. We are called to place our entire lives in the service of the Lord Jesus and His Church. In order for us to love, and follow the way of love, we have to know the truth and seek to follow the truth. In knowing, we can more greatly love.

This book is meant as a resource and field guide in the battle with the forces of darkness and sin. As the children of God, we are called to be the children of light. We do not accept the eclipses and shadows of sin in our fallen world. We do not accept ideologies based on brokenness or disorder. We do not compromise with evil. We labor to pursue divine wisdom. We die to ourselves so that we cooperate with divine grace. We speak truth. We suffer for goodness. We seek God's glory in all that we do!

As we follow the most excellent way of love, we are reminded that in receiving, we are also called to give. And so we accept with all our hearts the summons of the Lord Jesus to share His life and teachings.

"Go therefore and make disciples of all nations, baptizing them in the name of the Father and of the Son and of the Holy Spirit, teaching them to observe all that I have commanded you; and lo, I am with you always, to the close of the age."

—Matthew 28:19–20

Bibliography

General Sources

Catechism of the Catholic Church. Second Edition. 1997.
Compendium of the Social Doctrine of the Church. 2004.

Papal Sources

Pope John Paul II. *Address at Lourdes, France.* 2004.
———. *Airport Address.* Denver, CO. World Youth Day.
　　1993.
———. *Annual Message for World Immigration Day.* 1996.
———. Apostolic exhortation *Christifidelis Laici.* 1988.
———. *Apostolic letter Mulieris Dignitatem. 1988.*
———. Apostolic letter *Ordinatio Sacerdotalis.* 1994.
———. Encyclical *Centessimus Annus.* 1991.
———. Encyclical *Evangelium Vitae.* 1995.
———. Encyclical *Fides et Ratio.* 1998.
———. Encyclical *Laborem Exercens.* 1981.
———. Encyclical *Sollicitudo Rei Socialis.* 1987.
———. Encyclical *Veritatis Splendor.* 1993.
———. *World Day of Peace Message.* 1990.

Pope Benedict XVI. Encyclical *Caritas in Veritate.* 2009.
———. Encyclical *Deus Caritas Est.* 2005.

———. Encyclical *Spe Salvi*. 2007.

———. *Homily at Ordination of New Bishops*. 2009.

Magisterial Sources

Congregation for the Doctrine of the Faith. Instruction *Inter Insigniores*. 1976.

Other Sources

Martin Luther King Jr. *Letter from a Birmingham Jail*. 16 April 1963

———. *Speech at the Lincoln Memorial*. 28 August 1963.

Jeffrey Kirby. *Kingdom of Happiness: Living the Beatitudes in Everyday Life*. 2017.

———. *We Are the Lord's: A Catholic Guide to Difficult End-of-Life Questions*. 2019.

About the Author

F r. Jeffrey Kirby is pastor at Our Lady of Grace Catholic Church in the Diocese of Charleston in Indian Land, South Carolina. He is the author of several books, including *Kingdom of Happiness: Living the Beatitudes in Everyday Life*; *Doors of Mercy: Exploring God's Covenant with You*; and *Lord, Teach Us to Pray*. He has appeared on EWTN, Salt + Light television, and the BBC, as well as on Catholic radio.

He earned a bachelor's degree in history and a master's degree in philosophy from Franciscan University of Steubenville, where he also was given the 2017 John King Mussio Award for Faithful Service to the Church. Father Kirby also earned a bachelor's degree in sacred theology from the Pontifical Gregorian University. He has a master's degree in bioethics from the Pontifical Athenaeum Queen of the Apostles in Rome and a licentiate in moral theology from the Pontifical University of the Holy Cross in Rome, where he also earned a doctorate in sacred theology.